T0069106

CARTHA on Making Heimat was first published on the occasion of the 15th International Architecture Exhibition: La Biennale di Venezia as a contribution to the German Pavilion. The book was presented and exhibited in the German Pavilion in Venice's Giardini from August 28–31, 2016.

EDITORIAL
CARTHA

"This is the true nature of home – it is the place of peace: the shelters, not only from all injury, but from all terror, doubt and division…" John Ruskin, Sesame and Lilies

We want to focus on what we have in common rather than on what differentiates us from each other. Tzvetan Todorov's definition of otherness understood "as the relationship between people of different cultures and countries, as well as the otherness that binds you to the closest human beings", implies that the dependency relationships of human beings are constitutive of human identity, that the true human nature

resides in the common, not
in the special, that which makes
us different from each other is,
at its limit, accidental.

With this in mind, the relation
between acknowledging
others and the acknowledging
of oneself as part of the same
whole becomes clear. Thus,
if others are not at home, how
can we be?

When approaching the first
edition of CARTHA on *Making
Heimat*, it was our will
to extend this notion to the
contributions in order
to profit from their multi-
disciplinary background and
their diverse views on
the questions raised by the
German representation.
With this second edition we

wanted to expand on this,
to add a precise set of essays
and interviews that would
contribute to a better
understanding of the topic
at hand.

The copies displayed at the
German Pavilion served
their purpose within the context of the Venice Biennale
but they also made us
realise the potential in the
extension of the discussion
of their content beyond
the physical and temporal
limits of the Biennale.

This publication reflects
on migration movements and
their consequences, from
the perspective of otherness.
Whilst editing it, we
came to understand that one

valid way of creating the
space – not only physical but
also emotional and
conceptual – where "Heimat"
can be built, is through
the acknowledgement and
the awareness of others
and the relations that bind us.

AN EXCURSION INTO UNCHARTERED TERRITORY, THE STORY BEHIND MAKING HEIMAT, THE GERMAN CONTRIBUTION TO THE 2016 ARCHITECTURE BIENNALE IN VENICE

Oliver Elser
Peter Cachola Schmal
Anna Scheuermann

Making Heimat is growing. We feel delighted that our exhibition at the German Pavilion in Venice has inspired Cartha to do this special edition. But how did it all getting started?

The idea for Germany's contribution to the Architecture Biennale originated during the turbulent weeks of autumn 2015 when, every day, thousands of refugees were arriving at stations while the German Chancellor was sticking with an iron will to a policy of no upper limit for the number of refugees coming into the country. "Wir schaffen das" (We can do it). This unexpected openness became the Leitmotiv for the German Pavilion at the Biennale. Months later, the borders are again closed. By contrast, the German Pavilion is open. Four large new openings have been cut into the heritage listed façade.

Together with Something Fantastic – a Berlin based design office – and Clemens Kusch – an architect whose practice has for years now supervised all building and renovation work at the German Pavilion – we begin to draw up detailed plans for the location and size of the openings, plus the tender documents. The Federal Ministry for the Environment, Nature Conservation, Building and Nuclear Safety is persuaded to back the alterations. In official channels, everything is running like clockwork. Once the Milan consul hands over building application to the German Embassy in Rome, from where it goes to the Foreign Office, who asks the Construction Ministry what on earth is going on, it takes only a few days before two federal ministries have agreed to sign it off. The German Pavilion is to be opened up.

OPENNESS OR BUILDING SITE?

What precise message should the open pavilion try to convey? The Ministry's take on it is: since 2015, Germany has become a gigantic building site. By contrast, DAM and Something Fantastic feel the pavilion represents the friendly, open attitude towards all those streaming into Germany. Borders are open, walls are permeable – the country and the pavilion are no longer what they used to be. At the same time, the openings should not just reflect the current political situation, nor should they be a government-built statement sanctioning Merkel's strategy. The open pavilion should become a meeting place. It should no longer simply be an exhibition space, but a public space, a place flooded with light that draws visitors in. A space that scoops up the lagoon view through these huge openings, and brings it into the otherwise disconnected business of exhibition-making in the Giardini.

Had this idea been proposed for an Art Biennale, one might have said: 'OK, fine, let's leave it at that – mission fulfilled'. Would it not indeed suffice to cut open a heritage-listed building that still carries the burden of its Nazi past as well as all attempts at dealing that period, then deem it to be a huge sculpture, and simply leave it empty? Might that be a logical move? Or would such rigorous idealism just be terribly German? At an Art Biennale, an artist would need to throw their full weight behind such a radical gesture. In the Making Heimat project, Something Fantastic took on the role of the artist.

ETHNIC NETWORKS INSTEAD OF GHETTOS!
The Arrival City concept was there right from the start of the Biennale project. But opening up the pavilion was still a long way off. The refugee situation had by no means reached such epic proportions when DAM – with Doug Saunders – began their application process for the German pavilion in June 2015. By October 2015 the world had changed. The original idea of using Doug Sander's book as a springboard to examine what makes a successful Arrival City, and seek out Arrival Cities in Germany, had become eclipsed by the debate about the reception of refugees. However, to talk about Germany as a country of immigrants, rather than discuss the

role that architecture and urban planning might now play in helping to cope with the refugee crisis, would have been absurd. Under these circumstances, with so much palpable curiosity and enthusiasm, yet scepticism too, simply leaving the pavilion empty was clearly not an option either. As a result, the exhibition Making Heimat focused on two main issues. The first chapter showcases contemporary housing projects for refugees and in March 2016 a databank, which is continually updated, was set up on the website: makingheimat.de. The second chapter on-site in Venice addresses the question of what actually happens once a refugee becomes an immigrant. First studies indicate that when refugees leave their first officially assigned locality to move to cities, they tend to move to an Arrival City in which their fellow countrymen live. Rather than regarding these Arrival Cities as posing a danger, or as problem zones, ghettos or parallel societies, Doug Sander's book argues for a shift in perspective, regarding these places instead as offering immigrants an opportunity to start building a new life for themselves within existing immigrant networks.

The pavilion clearly bore the marks of those particular circumstances in autumn 2015, even though – with the closure of the Balkan route, and an agreement with Turkey concerning refugees – the political framework had already changed before the Biennale opened. As a result, by the time the pavilion finally opened to the public its overriding message had already become past history.

THE PAVILION WAS OPEN BUT
THE BORDERS WERE ALREADY CLOSED.
A STRANGE SITUATION.

During the Venice days, the space became a place for political manifestations that were banned elsewhere. For instance, a group of french activists presented their magazine at the German Pavilion because they were not allowed to do this in the nearby pavilion of France. So in it is best moments the pavilion was a platform. It was even taken as a starting point for this special issue of Cartha.

We appreciate the selection of authors for this publication. It might act as an intellectual backdrop for the more pragmatic, more 'reporting' approach of our Venice exhibition.

When we write down these lines, Making Heimat has come to Frankfurt. Coming back home, we took over a different task. Offenbach, an arrival city close to Frankfurt, is now in the focus. It is good to welcome those migrants, which were addressed as abstract subjects before, in our museum. At home we feel a different spirit. From the overview we have moved to the details of the everyday business of living together. The discussion can move on. Cartha and this special issue are a great contribution to this.

Saskia Sassen

Cartha – You have theorized about the incapacity of the term "migration" to define the current migration phenomena, incapable to grasp the nuances and complexities this entails. What could be a more appropriate way to define or refer to these current phenomena?

Saskia Sassen – There is a new type of migrant that is emerging from what I think of as a massive loss of habitat – this is a migrant who has no home that he/she leaves behind. This is a new type of refugee resulting from destructive forms of economic development and from climate change.[1]

Extreme violence is one key condition explaining these migrations. But so are thirty years of international development policies that have left much land dead (due to mining, land grabs, plantation agriculture) and expelled whole communities from their habitats.[2] Moving to the slums of large cities has increasingly become the last option, and for those who can afford it, migration. This multi-decade history of destructions and expulsions has reached extreme levels made visible in vast stretches of land and water bodies that are now dead. At least some of the localized wars and conflicts arise from these destructions, in a sort of "fight for habitat" and climate change further reduces livable ground. These are all issues I develop at length in "Expulsions". (published by Fisher Verlag – 2015)

Making Heimat addresses the question: "How can refugees and migrants who have left their familiar environments, settle and be 'at home'?" Which benefits do you think building and urban development can bring to refugees and migrants arriving in Germany? And which benefits might it bring to Germany?

Think of these migrants as usually well educated and trained, with skills, and the will to make a new life, precisely because there is no home to go back to as home is now a warzone, a mine, a plantation, a desert, a flooded plain. Think of these migrants as having the will to "make", that being to make an economy, make a culture, make a sociality. And then think of abandoned or semi-abandoned localities in Germany, and remember those migrants who have been offered to live in half empty or almost completely empty villages, and how they managed to make… yes, an economy, a culture, a sociality…[3]

Architecture and urbanism are disciplines that can take long periods of time to materialise. How can this inherent slow speed be managed in order for these disciplines to be relevant and helpful in dealing with the radical changes in migration matters?

What I described above is one way. This would be one option where architects, builders, water engineers, agricultural experts could help make it happen, and it would all add to the region, the country. I am also reminded of a group of techies, Spaniards, in one of Spain's major cities, I think it was Barcelona, who lost their jobs and decided to go into the arid mountains, to an abandoned village. It took

17

them two years and then they had a live economy, selling rural products to… guess what, the big cities in Spain.

What we do not want is what is happening increasingly in major cities – which is the buying of urban land by major corporations.[4/5]

Immigrants, with their capacity to make neighborhood economies, can be a major plus to resist this, though if a big firm really wants a plot of land they are ready for just about everything.

> Building and urban development play a key role in integration. Which concrete policies should be included in an urban development plan aimed at achieving a successful process of integration?

When we speak of urban environments – and not the under-inhabited environments I've described above – the picture becomes more complex. But one key fact that we know from the experience of so many immigrants across the world – from New York, to Nairobi, to Tokyo, is that immigrants, if allowed to live a normal life (not be secluded in camps) make jobs. Immigrants are famous for this: they make jobs, and if you live in any big German city you know that. The issue is the dying cities due to deindustrialization where jobs are being lost, and the residents feel that if immigrants came they would take away the few jobs that are left. There are mostly no immigrants in these cities, so its residents just know the fear of jobs, not what immigrants can do. They have a hard time imagining (and one can understand this) that if immigrants came, they would not take away jobs, because all they know is that the jobs keep disappearing from their cities. But if immigrants were given a chance to come, most of them would make jobs.

Which qualities are desirable for the public space of arrival cities? Are there any particular urban spaces or buildings that promote engagement and identification of the arriving migrants?

Public spaces, especially streets, are critical and I have a whole project on the street. I think of the street as an indeterminate space where even those who are not fully accepted can feel comfortable. The piazza, the boulevard, are overdetermined spaces and many newcomers, especially if immigrants and refugees, can easily feel that it is too overdetermined and really, even if public, are not "their" piazza or "their" boulevard. So alienation can set in. I am doing a project on this, a big project in Paris, supported by the College du Monde, a newly invented organization by Michel Wievorka which is quite exciting. And my husband, Richard Sennett is doing a parallel project there on Theatrum Mundi. So, back to your question, it has to be a mix of design, yes, but also the cultural, very broadly understood, background.[6]

What specific characteristics should social housing have in order to contribute to the integration of refugees and economic migrants?

Housing should also be a place for productive work – it cannot be reduced to sleeping and eating. The work that Teddy Cruz has done on this type of housing and neighborhood on the Mexico-US border is interesting. The larger setting or neighborhood where the housing is built should have streets that are public spaces, should have broad sidewalks and small squares where people mix, should have authorization for holding events, for making music, for teaching each other crafts and how to play instruments, so that it would draw all ages and locals and foreigners.

The idea of "integration through segregation" is recurrent in migration development discourses, arguing that migrants find it easier to settle if they share space with people from their same community of origin. Would you agree with that idea?

I think what should happen is what I have been describing above and small numbers matter, so multiple little squares and centers. This allows both immigrants to keep their culture, but also to share that culture and begin to share in the host culture, it is not a case of "either/or".

The cities are often unable to take quick architectural and urban decisions in order to handle the migrational fluxes. Could they go beyond both socio-economic global forces and government policies and return to local control?

De facto cities have had to engage in more local control because so much of our economies and hence politics are being urbanized. And yes, some of this authority should be formalized because that would justify central governments passing on more resources to cities.

20

The impact of the migration fluxes is usually analysed in the urban context, but what is the role of the countryside in the migratory phenomenon?

As I said earlier, we need to bring in the rural, especially in the form of under-inhabited villages, and even completely abandoned villages. If support for infrastructures can be mobilized, there will be significant numbers of migrants who will take on such possibilities and make it work.

New technologies have had a key role in many of the recent social revolutions. Are they also relevant in migrational processes?

Definitely: we have all heard from the recent flows of desperate people coming from the war zones that having their phones mattered a lot for a series of reasons, however much more could be done. All the items I have described above, that I think matter for incorporating migrants, should have a digital platform that can then also expand across a country and serve to help and inform on situations where matters are not going well. I have worked on some of this for the case of low-income neighborhoods in major cities in the US. Also interesting is the notion of open-sourcing the neighborhood.[7]

The process of "making heimat" is to be accomplished by both the arrival country and the immigrants themselves. What role do you think refugees and migrants should play in their process of integration?

I think I have answered this above, but let me add also that the migrant should be allowed to keep parts of her culture and should be invited to learn about local cultures for example in local weekend street or small square events, where small groups of locals and foreigners can actually mix. To help this there should be a central activity that can be share like music making, where everybody brings an instrument, including a pot that can be a drum, or your voice, is often something that works well. Events around cooking is another example when understood as cooking plus talking about food, demonstrating to each other, and above all, eating together. Participants should be old, young, both men and women and should always be in small numbers. When the 2000 crisis hit in Argentina, I remember in Buenos Aires fired workers re-entered abandoned factories and opened them up to the community.[8] They kept part of the space for working and selling what they had done before under a boss, and the rest of the space was for the community where they would meet and cook collectively etc., and it worked!

1 http://sur.conectas.org/en/three-emergent-migrations-epochal-change/
2 http://socdev.ucpress.edu/content/2/2/204
3 https://www.theguardian.com/world/2013/oct/12/italian-village-migrants-sea
4 http://www.theguardian.com/cities/2015/nov/24/who-owns-our-cities-and-why-this-urban-takeover-should-concern-us-all
5 We also did a fairy tale version, your readers might enjoy: http://www.theguardian.com/cities/2015/dec/23/monster-city-urban-fairytale-saskia-sassen?CMP=twt—gu
6 "The Global Street or the Democracy of the Powerless" http://kulturaliberalna.pl/2012/02/20/the-global-street-or-the-

democracy-of-the-powerless/
and
"The Global Street: Making the Political"
http://www.tandfonline.com/doi/full/10.1080/14747731.
2011.622458
7   http://www.forbes.com/sites/techonomy/2013/11/10/
open-sourcing-the-neighborhood/
and
http://www.livemint.com/Specials/m21w1rzMM8KpbE-
9KO1iFVK/Redefining-notions-of-urban-intelligence.html
8   "fabricas ocupadas"

PROPERTY OBLIGES
Brandlhuber+

The text Property Obliges is based on an interview as part of the ongoing film project *Legislating Architecture*, by Brandlhuber+ Christopher Roth.

A discussion on the openness of society is always about the accessibility of space for people – a priori.

This inevitably leads to the debate about the right of usage and in our current setting to the question of "who owns the ground?".

The issue of appropriation of ground is basic for all forms of migration, including our own.

Thus, the question of land ownership is the starting point in the possible transition to an open city, country and Society.

§14 Basic Law for the Federal Republic of Germany / sentence 2 Property entails obligations. Its use shall also serve the public good.[1]

The German Federal Constitutional Court expresses its stance on Article 14 of the Basic Law in a decree from January, 12th 1967. It refers to the protocols of the Parliamentary Council of 1948, which clearly show that the second sentence of Article 14 of the Basic Law was designed with the matter of landed property in mind. Accordingly, regarding questions of ownership of land and property, the Federal Constitutional Court is obliged to the interests of the general public to a far greater extent than regarding other property assets. The fact that the use of land is unavoidable and indispensable, shall prohibit it from being left to the inestimable free play of market forces and to the discretion of the individual.[2]

Subsequently, thoughts from a dialogue between Dr. Hans-Jochen Vogel and Arno Brandlhuber should provide an impulse for reflection on this topic. Hans-Jochen Vogel (SPD, Social Democratic Party) former Mayor of Munich (1960–72), Federal Minister for Regional Planning, Building and Urban Development (1972–74), Federal Minister of Justice (1974–81) and Governing Mayor of Berlin (1981), inter alia focuses on questions of landownership and their direct link to the German Basic Law as well as the levy of unjustified land assets. Vogel envisions a land management which enforces ecological and social objectives in municipal and regional spatial planning.[3]

Article 14 discloses the still unresolved tension between the rule of law and the welfare state. The social injustices which are caused by the rapid rise of land prices to a significant degree, affect us all. According to Vogel, in Munich, the land price has increased by 36.000 per cent over the last fifty years. Consequently, therefore, he not only raises the question of affordable housing but also of unpredictable expenses for municipalities when buying land for necessary infrastructure and building projects.

The profiteers of this upward spiral are landowners, who themselves do not provide any services like investments in reutilization or infrastructure. Profits from land ownership largely derive from the growing demand for land or from taxpayers' investments in infrastructure. Vogel does not see any justification for the enormous revenues of this small group of fortunate landowners.

In this respect, Hans-Jochen Vogel provides a first approach to solve the problem of steadily increasing land prices and the privatization of land, by suggesting the division of land ownership rights into usage-rights and freehold-rights: "The existing ownership of land is divided into usage and freehold property – whereby the latter would belong to the community. It establishes a contractual right of usage, which can be terminated or granted only for a limited time and regulates the nature and duration of the use, as well as the usage-fee. If this is not in conflict with communal interests, the usage-right is to be awarded by public tender."[4]

This new property management would restore the flexibility needed to meet the challenges we are facing today. A dynamic urban development that is beneficial to all groups of society, first and foremost requires a mobile land management that can adapt to social realities.

The idea of a new land management was a recurring matter for Social Democrats as well as for other parties. In 1989, this important debate became a topic of political discussion and part of Berlin's SPD's policy program. Since then, however, the discussion about a potential reform has died down, and disappeared completely from the political debate.

1   Basic Law for the Federal Republic of Germany
    §14 Basic Law, Sentence 2
2   Protocols of the parliamentary council: ParlRat, 8th meeting
    of the Committee of Basicists, Sten.Prot. P. 62ff.
3   Policy statement of the Social Democratic Party, decided by
    the party conference of the Social Democratic Party of
    Germany on December 20th, 1989 in Berlin changed at the
    partie's conference in Leipzig on April 17th, 1998
4   From „Neue Juristische Wochenschrift" 1972, vol. 35,
    p. 1544ff, reprinted in Dialogic City – Berlin wird Berlin;
    Cologne, 2015, pp. 651ff

Giovanna Borasi

Cartha – In the *Journeys* exhibition with the great title, *How Travelling Fruits, Ideas and Buildings Rearrange our Environment*, you approach the topic of migration as something inherent to our nature. Migration is, after all, a constant in human history. My question would be, how do you perceive the current situation regarding migration in the Mediterranean Sea?

Giovanna Borasi – I curated this show in 2010, and I think the context was very different then. This sense of emergency was maybe already present, especially in the Mediterranean area, but it was years before we came to have a kind of critical flow at this pace. The idea was to look at migration as an inherent part of human history. When I decided to work on this topic, I realized there have been many exhibitions and research projects that dealt with the flow of people: how people move from one place to another, how many immigrants a country has and so on. Beyond the basic fact that people move, I was more interested in what the tangible consequences of these displacements would be with respect to architecture and the built environment. What are the traces and the inevitable cultural changes that this movement implies? More than responding to the question, "How do we deal with this emergency?" the exhibition addressed some key aspects of what migration means and, more specifically, the idea of people moving with cultural baggage like techniques of building that a community brings from one culture to another. How do these techniques influence the new place and what is the impact in the long term? I think it is also important to mention that this show took place in the context of Canada, where migration has a certain meaning. It is very different from the European situation. And it is very different from the United States, where there is the idea of the melting pot, where, in the end, everybody becomes American and the previous culture is set aside. In Canada, the idea is that your own culture stays with you. Even if you enter into a set of Canadian values, your own culture and identity are still very much respected.

Today we realize that Europe is the destination for many migrants. The amount of people arriving is critical. How then are these people integrated and helped? How do we deal with all of these questions? So the show – and the title alludes to this – tried not to be specific to a certain time or certain flows of migrations, but to tackle the more general and universal issues caused by these flows. Quite deliberately, a human body was not represented in the exhibition. I was always referring, in a metaphorical way or in an abstract way, to ideas moving through building techniques, ideas of architecture, or even fruits and vegetables. Basically the intention was to address these topics, referring always to our human history, but never really to relate directly to a certain group of people or to a specific set of cultures. For me, it was very much about, for example, people moving from Italy to Vermont because they were particularly skilled in working with granite. And they

29

changed the culture in the area around Barre, Vermont: many of the migrants were anarchists, and in Vermont today there are still many institutions that are very much left leaning. This development can be traced to this period of migration. So it was not just about these Italians coming to Vermont with their expertise in carving; they also brought their political ideas that had an influence in certain communities.

So if I return to your question about what is happening today, I think the conditions are very different. I feel we are facing an emergency. We have to deal with a situation that we perhaps aren't prepared for and do not have good answers for. It's tempting to propose an immediate answer to respond to what is happening today. In addition, we have a Europe that doesn't have a unified idea of how to deal with issues of migration. In the Mediterranean, historically populations coexist with flows and continuous cultural exchanges. For example, the story I wrote for the book that accompanies the exhibition – which is not a series of essays or academic case studies but rather fictional writings – I focused on Mazara del Vallo, a small town in Sicily where the language is mixed with Arabic due to centuries of exchange with Tunisia. Italians fished in Tunisian waters, and vice versa. This has changed the town's culture and has also left traces in the built environment and structure of the town, where the main core has distinct Arab characteristics. I think there is a very different approach in countries that are at the edge of the Mediterranean. I would say that in Greece, Italy, Portugal, and Spain, there is an understanding of migration that is different from the understanding of the issue elsewhere in Europe. I think the emergency now is happening in a Europe that is certainly not unified in its approach; each country deals with local policies in a distinct way.

> I would like to go back to what you referred before, to these anarchists who moved to Vermont, that they somehow brought with them their culture. This refers to the concept of "Making Heimat" – it's not a one-way road, it has to be a two-way, so the country somehow accommodates the people, but the people also implicitly have an influence over the country. How do you think building and urban development can be beneficial to refugees and migrants at their arrival cities? Is this two-way event at all possible or is it an utopia?

As I said I think now we are treating situations like this as emergencies. For immigrants, there is a city where they first arrive, where they are helped at the first level. But then there is no clear vision of a future and how they can be integrated into society. There are also many people who arrive in a country but actually want to reach another European country. Can we say these people are choosing to migrate to this first country as if they wanted to stay, or are they just escaping? This is just the first place they land; any safe place is fine from this perspective.

At the CCA last year, we had a show on two projects by Álvaro Siza from the 1980s that address this

31

question of the integration of migrants, in the context of Berlin and The Hague. Siza remarked that the Dutch government asked him to design two different types of housing: one for Dutch people and one for Turkish migrants. But he refused to comply with this, as he thought it was a sign of a double segregation. The immigrants would never really be integrated if the attitude is, "You are Turkish, so you live in an apartment that is tailored – supposedly – to your culture." The migrants will always be different because they will never have the opportunity to understand what living in the Netherlands is really like. I have to say that I find this idea of defining a specific architecture or a specific part of the city as dedicated to an incoming population extremely problematic in the long term. I understand there is an emergency – all these people have to live somewhere – but I don't think is the way to solve the problem.

In the *Journeys* exhibition we also had an example that focused on a Dutch urban context: the Bijlmermeer, a modern neighbourhood of Amsterdam that promised a very pleasant life. But when in the 1970s the people of Suriname (a former colony of the Netherlands) were offered Dutch passports and the possibility to move to the Netherlands, there was a sudden migration to Amsterdam. As the government didn't really know where to put all these people, the Bijlmermeer became an immediate answer: it transformed very quickly from a modern, white, middle-class neighbourhood to a Surinamese ghetto. It is interesting to see how this community used Bloemenoord – a modern building in the Bijlmermeer with a structure similar to l'Unité. The immigrants immediately started to densely occupy and use the building's corridors for markets and other public functions. So it became an animated city. The government, preoccupied with how to deal with this kind of new ghetto, decided to impose a very precise percentage of the kind of people admitted. A maximum of 30 percent of the residents could be of foreign origin. This became a very racial program, concerning what was considered the "healthiest" percentages of different communities possible to maintain a kind of Dutch livability. It's interesting to see how the migrants used the Bloemenoord megastructure in a very creative way (maybe even in a way that was nearer to the project's initial intentions), but also to see how this structure transformed itself quickly into an arrival city for the migrants, pushing out the previous inhabitants.

And this dealing with the percentage of people from each countries, did it work in some positive way? What were the outcomes of this?

I think it was just a bureaucratic strategy to regulate an "acceptable mix", but I don't think it really worked. The Bijlmermeer is now a more elitist neighbourhood again because of the quality of the apartments and so on, but there were a lot of discussions about this solution. It was in fact a very top-down experiment.

In Europe, I think there's no parallel. There's no model for it. But, if we compare it to the volume of migration, for instance, in South America, in Brazil, with internal migrations of rural exodus, that people just escaped to São Paulo and Rio, there was this huge governmental programme of housing on the cities outskirts. For instance, the famous City of God, that still exists today. This structure, that was supposed to be temporary, became something completely permanent, altered and appropriated by the communities that moved in. If the German government is imposing this kind of limit, it might seem safe to say the this will not happen there.

If we look at the problem from a social perspective, we could say that there is always a sort of "good intention" that covers all of these housing programs. So then the responses are similar to what the Red Cross or other similar organizations do after an earthquake. What are the immediate priorities? Giving these people a roof over their heads, for example. And so any answer is fine as long as shelter is provided. But if you start to look at this from a different perspective, if you consider the city as your problem and not just the people (let's forget about the people for a moment), then you might find other answers and other strategies. If you look from the point of view of the city, you might ask, "What is right for the city?" The new condition is that many migrants are arriving, so most probably we have to expand city structures and we have to develop our urban system. What is the right way to do this? In the past, cities dealt with this question by adding to the existing texture, augmenting the density.

34

I think it is important to challenge the current mindset that tends to create a set of different conditions for the newcomers; the understanding is they will stay in a temporary way. We must take the city's point of view and imagine how to deal with this. What should be the answer? A denser urban tissue, more building, more satellite communities, or new cities? I'm not aware of any discussion of this sort these days. For me, the real question is: if this is the current situation and Europe gets these additional millions of people, how will you face this, beyond the social emergency, focusing on how the model of the city might adapt to such rapid growth? That, for me, is the interesting discussion, to take this crisis as an opportunity to change urban settlements and their structure.

But somehow, the justification offered by the German pavilion take on the situation, was contradictory to this. According to the "Arrival cities" conclusions, precisely because there are no other people that came to these areas previously from these countries where these people are coming from, they will not move there, they will not want to go there. Rem Koolhaas did a comment on this. He said exactly what you said now; "why not direct or indicate these people that are migrating into Germany that they should go to these areas where they would have these opportunities, housing, etc." This is connected to the next point I would like to introduce; We pretty much talk about cities as the only situation influenced by migration. In the *Journeys* exhibition, some of the essays also went into the influence of migrations on the countryside. How do you see these two realities?

35

First of all, I would like to draw attention to the character of the countryside nowadays, especially in Europe where it is a very urbanized place. Often it's the place where there is a lot of work to be done and where many workers end up finding jobs. Some years ago there was an advertisement from the Minister of Internal Affairs in Italy, which tried to counteract a kind of racist, right-wing attitude. These ads showed all the things that you, as an Italian, would not have if migrants were not there to produce them. So forget about Parmesan cheese; that is produced by immigrant Sikh communities who take care of the cows. Forget about tomatoes and oranges. You would think, "This is my culture" but in fact it's all managed by migrants. I agree with you: we focus a lot on this very old idea that everybody moves to cities because that is where the jobs are and where there is a concentration of everything. But I think the countryside is an interesting place to look at in terms of how these immigrant communities can be integrated, how they find opportunities for work and a different kind of integration with the local communities. In this sense, there is a very interesting situation in Canada now, and I think the government has a problem with it. Many small Canadian communities have decided to invite Syrian refugees to live. So these small communities in the middle of nowhere, in the Canadian prairies, raised money to, let's say, adopt these families. It's a very different attitude; people, as a community, decide to welcome immigrants and confront the need to think about how to handle these people once they arrive. I gather that in the countryside, this would very much be possible. I think this could be the topic for one of the next shows at the CCA: the idea of the countryside as a place where a lot of new technologies have been developed, and where social experiments have been carried out. AMO/OMA is working on this, and in Japan there is a new tendency to consider going back to the countryside because of the growth of the aging population. It is very specific – there is virtually no migration in Japan – but the country is facing the issue of an aging population in areas that are completely abandoned because the young population wants to live in big cities and to be connected to a completely different condition. Therefore, there are very interesting projects being developed now to try to understand how to bring communities and work back to the countryside. I think that, in Europe, this is not happening at the level of policy but it is happening simply because of the fact that a lot of people find jobs in the countryside. But in these cases housing and living conditions are not really addressed.

BRINGING IT ALL BACK HOME
Alfredo Brillembourg
Hubert Klumpner
Alexis Kalagas

Migration is a defining challenge for architects and designers today. But migration has always been at the heart of urban change. Cities are fundamentally places of opportunity – urban migrants continue to be drawn in their millions by the promise of security as well as upward mobility. As Doug Saunders has suggested, the unprecedented urbanization patterns to which we bear witness are, at their core, an epic story of human movement, set in motion by the common search for a better life.[1] The "migration crisis" that burned so brightly in the collective European consciousness for months in 2016 before being overtaken by fears of violence and "homegrown" terrorism represents just one chapter in this story. But far from a simple narrative of unanticipated arrivals exposing chinks in the armor of fortress Europe, as architects and designers we must understand our role in the refugee "crisis" in broader terms. It is a role that spans countries and continents.

A HOUSE IS NOT A HOME
In the last year, European architectural discourse and activism has been dominated by a simple humanitarian impulse – the need for fast and effective

emergency shelter in cities and towns struggling to cope with an influx of newcomers. Exhibitions like *Making Heimat*, however, allude to more intangible questions that resist a design quick fix. What exactly makes a built environment feel like home? What material deprivation and sense of danger must be experienced to push someone to flee that home? How can a person continue to retain a sense of identity and connection to a wider community as they move in fits and starts through unfamiliar landscapes and territories? Does the process of settling in a new city – however long – necessarily lead to the establishment of a new home? And after years of conflict, destruction, and absence, is it possible to return "home" and rediscover what was lost in a place that has been rendered unrecognizable?

For those engaged with the full reality of the refugee issue these are challenging questions and impossible to ignore. Rather than a linear journey from A to B, ending with successful long-term integration into a welcoming "host" society, forced migration is often a circular phenomenon. Architects and designers have crucial roles to play in the places that migrants leave, the spaces through which they travel, the urban environments where they will attempt to build new homes, and the transformed cities, towns, and villages to which they may eventually return. Our recent edition of *SLUM Lab* magazine is dedicated to this theme, and explores the way in which conflict urbanism, internal displacement camps, border fortifications, liminal settlements, informal transit camps, planned camps, detention centers, reception centers, first step housing, social housing, and various phases of post conflict reconstruction each reveal the way built space shapes, and is reshaped by, the refugee experience.[2]

IDENTITY AND ARCHITECTURE
At Urban-Think Tank, we have also engaged with some of these questions in our design projects. On a conceptual level, our involvement in Hello Wood's annual design-build workshop "Project Village" has explored ideas of temporariness and collectivity. Most recently, the "Migrant Hous(ing)" project grew from the desire to devise a structure that was itself migrant in nature. Each individual arrived to the site with an individual unit – a series of rotating frames that could configure into a multitude of spaces based on personal need. These units had material limitations that prevented individuals from building complete solitary housing. As they began to form relationships, however, the units transformed. Only through a collective force could they fulfill their structural potential and exert their limitless combinatorial possibilities, testing the true nature of community building. The project questioned how displaced individuals begin to establish relationships with other traveling migrants, and whether architecture can preserve individual identity while contributing to integration.

More concretely, our Empower Shack housing project in Cape Town is, at its heart, a response to
40

the long-term struggle of migrants to establish a foothold in a new city. In this case, however, the pattern in question is rural-to-urban, rather than the fraught cross-border route traced by refugees (though South Africa continues to attract those fleeing violence and persecution across the continent).[3] In many ways, Khayelitsha is a classic "arrival city". But the particularities of post-apartheid urbanism, combined with persistent barriers to effective informal settlement upgrading, mean even after 20 years most residents of our pilot site in BT-Section live in a perpetual state of tenure insecurity and spatially entrenched poverty. Pulled by family networks and pushed by the promise of a better life, the community – transplanted largely from the Eastern Cape – has found itself disconnected from public services and employment opportunities. The "home" they have forged is fragile, marginal, and rife with personal dangers and environmental risks.

The aim of Empower Shack is to develop a scalable settlement upgrading methodology that offers immediate access to dignified shelter and basic services while establishing a clear pathway to incremental formalization. The project integrates community participation, a new housing prototype, spatial planning, and urban systems that contribute to a sustainable economic model and new livelihood opportunities. Beyond meeting immediate needs, the project also has symbolic value. The post-apartheid South African constitution enshrined a "right of access to adequate housing". But this bureau-

41

cratic language masks the deeper promise – an end to deliberate structural inequality and exclusion, where the idea of "home" was contingent on the whims of government planners and strictly circumscribed. For refugees and internal migrants alike, the ability to integrate goes hand in hand with the ability to imagine and build a brighter future. In its fullest sense, this means the ability to participate in a city's political, economic and social life.

Visiting Khayelitsha, it becomes immediately apparent that the lived experience of most South Africans is not reflected in existing planning approaches. Until now, the residents of BT-Section have had no dialogue with formal planning provisions. By accepting the need to work with what already exists – however shaped by a history of discrimination – we have been able to negotiate with the City of Cape Town to employ more permanent construction techniques and materials, allowing the upgraded homes to eventually join the formal housing stock. Greater certainty about tenure security and future adherence to housing codes will not only overcome the paralyzing effect of "permanent impermanence", but also encourage incremental investment in an asset now recognized by financial institutions. The initial phase, consisting of four adjoining houses to the south of the main site, was completed in December 2015 and is currently undergoing user evaluation. The next phase will commence in May 2017, including the roll out of 72 additional units.

As Europeans decamped *en masse* for beaches in Greece, Italy, France, and Spain in July last year to escape the summer heat, more migrants than ever before were dying attempting to cross the Mediterranean.[4] In the meantime, the March resettlement deal hurriedly agreed between Turkey and the European Union had seen land borders across the continent slam shut. The conflicts in Syria, Afghanistan, and elsewhere responsible for fuelling a persistent wave of refugees continued, but Europe was closed for business. At the opening of the Biennale that May, the world of architecture descended upon the labyrinthine canals and alleys of Venice under the guise of "reporting from the front". Designers were called upon to fight "the battles that need[ed] to be fought". But if urbanization is ultimately a story of migration, then the frontlines of architecture have always been located along the shifting routes and in the liminal zones traversed by people seeking a new home.

Skip forward a year, and the global community is older, but not wiser. From the shoot-from-the-hip executive orders of the Trump administration, to the rising populist tide in France, the Netherlands, and, indeed, South Africa, resurgent nationalism and xenophobia have seen the notion of an inclusive "Heimat" open to, and tolerant of, newcomers fade. It would be foolish to suggest that architecture alone holds the answers. But the built environment cannot be divorced from the context in which it was

43

produced. Our towns and cities hold up a mirror to both our best and worst impulses. Whether in the sprawling refugee settlements of Kakuma or Zaatari, the squalid basement apartments of central Athens, the makeshift encampments connecting the fluid "Balkan route", or the restive immigrant enclaves of Stockholm, Berlin, or Brussels, we all have a role to play in meeting the complex spatial challenge posed by unprecedented flows of humanity. The moral demands are rather more straightforward.

1   Doug Saunders, *Arrival City: How the Largest Migration in History is Reshaping Our World* (2010).
2   Alexis Kalagas (ed), *SLUM Lab 11: Forced Migration* (2017).
3   Stephen Lawrence Gordon, 'Welcoming Refugees in the Rainbow Nation: Contemporary Attitudes Towards Refugees in South Africa' (2016) 35 *African Geographical Review*.
4   Lizzie Dearden, 'Refugee Crisis: 2016 on Course to be the Deadliest Year on Record as Thousands of Asylum Seekers Drown in Mediterranean', *The Independent* (30 July 2016).

David Harvey

Cartha – The design and planning of physical urban spaces is deemed crucial prior to the arrival of new migrations. How can architecture and urban development contribute to the integration of refugees and economic migrants in arrival cities?

David Harvey – Migrants and refugees bring with them a whole host of cultural presumptions, habits, religious beliefs and forms of sociality – e.g. of family and kinship). While it is not the duty of any receiving country to replicate such conditions (an impossibility in any case when refugees come from multiple and very diverse backgrounds – some sensitivity has to be shown to the idea of creating footholds within an existing urban fabric for creative integration and self-management of the spaces in which people live and eventually find and create employment opportunities. There is no formula for this, but close working with migrants and refugees on the ground and coming up with experimental designs can be exciting as well as challenging work.

You oppose two concepts when theorizing about the urban phenomena: the processes of urbanization and the Lefebvrian concept of "the right to the city", which you claim as a freedom to make and remake our cities and ourselves. Could you explain the differences between these two concepts?

The theory of urbanization is an attempt to show how the laws of motion of capital and capital accumulation are involved in city building. The aim is the maximization of accumulation of capital (along with the maximization of land values and rent extractions) no matter what. The trend is to create cities for people (particularly privileged elites) to invest in and not necessarily cities for the popular classes to live in. The right to the city views this same process from the standpoint of the popular classes where the aim is to create decent living environments for all through democratic forms of governance. Obviously these two visions clash and the struggle over the right to the city ensues.

You claim that urban development is intertwined with a social class struggle logic. Could you provide us of some examples of how this is reproduced in urban geographies?

The eviction of low-income populations from whole neighborhoods in favored locations to make way for megaprojects or higher value land uses favored by financiers, developers and construction interests is almost everywhere in evidence.

How has the 20th century European processes of urbanization, consisting of important migrations of population to urban areas, contributed to the erosion of local aesthetics?

I don't see the intrusion of alternative aesthetic preferences and judgments as necessarily bad. Indeed, I find the local differentiations created through migratory movements far preferable to monotonous and boring developer urbanization. The real estate development lobby often destroys character whereas anarchists, squatters and cultural workers along with immigrants often play a role in creating a much more interesting urban fabric. It is not always so of course but here too it is the dynamics of open struggle that should be allowed to flourish.

> The role of property markets seems to have played a role in urban plan designs. Has urbanism operated under the umbrella of these designs?

One of the biggest unsolved and underdiscussed aspects of urbanization is the role of property markets in general and private property markets in particular in shaping urban life. I believe a great deal of effort must now be put into designing alternative property arrangements, common property regimes, and other ways of securing people's rights in the city.

> To date, migration policies are exclusively the responsibility of state, but some local governments are building transnational alliances to bypass the state's competencies. Do you foresee a scenario in which the transnational alliances between urban centers overcomes the state-nation power?

I think transnational alliances at the local scale are an excellent idea but I don't see this supplanting relations developing at broader scales and that will certainly involve some level of interaction like that of the state.

> Would it be possible to incorporate the refugee and migrants voice into policy making decisions that concern migrations? Through which channels could this happen?

The self-organization of refugee groups should be a priority. Assembly style self-governance would

> To what extent are the processes of migration aligned with the urbanization processes?

They are never "aligned" but always a productive, disruptive and potentially creative force.

> Could these migrational processes be an opportunity to change social housing policies? How can social housing help in the process of integration of economic migrants and refugees?

The advent of a crisis of refugees and migrants creates many stresses at the same time as it offers opportunities to explore new forms of social housing, with the emphasis upon the nature of the sociality involved. Training migrants in construction so they can self-build their own communal housing would seem a good idea. Too often migration is seen as a problem whereas historically it has more often than not turned out to be a great opportunity.

> "Smart cities" and "business parks" seems to dominate the new language of modern cities. What can we expect in the digital era of ICT in terms of urbanism?

I am all in favor of the kinds of explorations that improve the efficiency of movement and social provision in urban settings and the mining of big data sets and the pursuit of Smart city agendas is helpful. Unfortunately, if this is all there is then the results will be disastrous. Smart City thinking cannot get at the radical transformation of social relations

48

and of practices required to turn our cities into eminently liveable environments in which everyone has the right to decent housing provision in decent living environments. Smart city thinking cannot challenge the habit of big capital to build cities to invest in but not to live in. Smart city thinking leads to the illusion that solutions to global poverty and environmental degradation lie in new technologies. This has never worked in the past and I see no reason why the pursuit of some techno-utopia will succeed in the future. We need a right to the city movement grounded in an anti-capitalist ethic if we are to succeed in the quest for better urban living for all.

What does it mean to adopt a critical position towards urbanism theory?
Question the authority of received wisdom and conventional practices and make sure that the transformation of social relations in constructive ways is the central motif rather than technocratic and bureaucratic preferences.

Iverna McGowan

Cartha – According to the UNHCR, over 60% of the world's 19.5 million refugees and 80% of 34 million Internal Displaced People (IDPs) live in urban environments. What are the main causes that underpin forced displacements?

Iverna McGowan – Very often the causes for internal displacement are the same as those which cause people to flee across borders. Take Afghanistan as an example, the intensifying conflict there has taken a devastating toll on civilians. As of April 2016, a staggering 1.2 million people were displaced within the country. This is a substantial increase compared to the end of 2012, when these numbers stood at almost 500.000. In the first four months of 2016 alone, 118.000 people had fled their homes of whom approximately 80% required emergency humanitarian assistance – this is an average of nearly one thousand newly displaced people per day. Other causes can also lead to internal displacement such as economic crises, drought, famine etc. One of the challenges that IDP[1] can face is that there is a risk of deprioritisation of responding to their plight as they are still within their own country and therefore are often not seen as obviously in need of humanitarian relief as refugee camps which are in other countries. In Afghanistan the conditions of IDPs remain woefully inadequate partly due to the governments political difficulties and to the fact that international donors have not yet put enough

50

focus on the needs of IDPs when looking at longer term strategies for Afghanistan.

The role of Amnesty International in a refugee crisis is extremely complex due to the existence of different levels of crisis, from emergency rescues to policy-making advising. In this regard, what are the main challenges that face Amnesty International to date?
We must be very clear that when we talk about Europe there is no refugee crisis. There is a crisis of politics, policy and humanity perhaps but in terms of tangible numbers arriving there is no refugee crisis in Europe. There are currently some 20 million refugees worldwide. The vast majority are hosted in low and middle income countries, while many of the world's wealthiest nations host the fewest and do the least. We cannot in the EU, the world's wealthiest political bloc with a population of over 500 million people, rationally explain why 50,000 refugees remain stranded in Greece in appalling conditions, nor why the resettlement figures into the EU remain so painfully low. All this is to say that the most challenging thing for Amnesty International in this context is the lack of political leadership. Mainstream political leaders, also at EU level, are pandering to extremists and trying to support the idea that there are no other options left other than to abandon international obligations and damn millions of people to misery.

Earlier this year Amnesty International conducted the Refugees Welcome Index[2] which ranked 27 countries across all continents based on people's

51

willingness to let refugees live in their countries, towns, neighbourhoods and homes. The results were staggering with four in five people saying that they would welcome refugees to their country. It seemed that UK and Australian governments were more out of touch than any other leaders globally: an astonishing 87% of British people and 85% of Australians are ready to invite refugees into their countries, communities – even their own homes. So although we see on an individual human level inspiring levels of compassion from ordinary people, lazy political leaders instead use their own people's lack of willingness as an excuse and even try and pin their own political failings as leaders on refugees and migrants. That is one of the largest challenges we face. Of course the sheer scale of the global crisis with more people on the move since the Second World War also means that we have to work around the clock to monitor, report on and challenge new harmful policies and practices as we see them when it comes to refugees. The scale on which to do this poses its own challenges.

Germany has been the EU country which has by far received the highest number of asylum applications in 2015, with more than 476,000. What benefits do you think can be brought to German society itself by building and urban development that is focused towards refugee and migrant integration?

This is not something we would have official commentary on.

> Some scholars argue that homogeneity within neighbourhoods makes it easier for refugees to feel 'at home', thus facilitating migrant and refugee integration to the arrival country. What pros and cons do you think segregation can have for people trying to settle?

Segregation is highly problematic, look for example at the treatment of the Roma people in many countries across Europe. In many countries (EU has opened infringement proceedings against Czech Rep. and Slovakia for this) Roma children face segregation in education. Equal access to housing and education let's not forget are human rights. It will be vitally important also in the case of refugees and migrants that a strong anti-discrimination approach is used to ensure that segregation and the potential accompanying rights violations are avoided.

> Making Heimat addresses the idea of creating a "new home" for refugees who have left their familiar environments. In short, it underlines the importance of an integration process. To what extent could resettlement contribute to the successful of a process of integration?

It is challenging enough for anyone to move to a new place, new culture, new language often away from networks of family and friends. Refugees have often fled very traumatising situations and therefore its desirable that they receive further assistance to help their transition such as counselling, training etc. Resettlement processes when done properly can hugely help in this way by speeding up and facilitating the transition process, this can also (depending

53

also on whether they are allowed to work) increase the transition time to economic self-sufficiency and integration into society.

Do you think a temporary "Heimat" is possible?
Having studied German philosophy and culture at University I understand that the German word "Heimat" carries with it an emotional weight, going beyond the physical place of home to the broader psychological and cultural links to a social unit. Myself an Irish person living in Belgium, and having lived in many other countries over the past number of years I do believe indeed that a temporary Heimat is possible. Home as we say in English is where the heart is, so once you are willing to emotionally and intellectually invest in the place where you find yourself you can build a sense of Heimat in that place. Making new friendships and social connections is vital to this process I believe.

Amnesty International collaborates with Forensic Architecture, a research agency that provides advanced architectural and media research to legal and political forums. How can architecture contribute to making migrant and refugee needs visible?
Indeed Amnesty International collaborates with a research agency to use Forensic Architecture to document and analyse breaches of international humanitarian law and human rights law. It allows us even in densely populated urban areas, for example in the case of bombings, to dissect and model dynamic events as they unfold to ensure that evidence

of any international crimes are fully recorded. With regard to refugees of course it is often conflict that they are fleeing. We hope by using this evidence in the long-run that there can be justice and accountability for breaches of international humanitarian law and therefore a reduction going forward in such violations in the future which would hopefully lead to a reduction in the number of those who need to flee in the first place.

More broadly architecture can be used to remind us all of the stories of migration from our own histories or reflect current events. Often in European countries you can see a historical trace of the migration history through the buildings that still stand. Whether it's the relics of ancient Roman buildings in northern Europe or the beautiful gardens of the Real Alcázar Palace in Spain we can see how movement of different people through generations has influenced in beautiful ways our surroundings. This should serve as a reminder that the phenomenon of people moving is as old as human history itself and perhaps challenges some of the irrationally fearful narratives we hear today on the 'dangers' of migration. Marvelling at architecture brought to Europe by different cultures can also serve as a positive enforcement of the richness that a more diverse society can bring.

The 1951 Refugee Convention is said to be outdated. What changes could boost refugees' empowerment and autonomy?

The Convention is not outdated, it is extremely currently relevant. The problem is the lack of political will and leadership in today's world to hold up the Conventions noble ambitions and to respect the rights that people hold under it. When we look at what is happening on the ground in Greece at the moment, we must despair. Men, women and children including elderly people, sick people and pregnant women are forced to live in circumstance that are not fit for the human person. Nothing is undermining their autonomy and empowerment more than this dehumanising treatment. It is vital that their needs and voices are directly listened to by policy makers. All too often at the moment political deals are made which will have huge consequences on peoples' lives with little thought for what the people themselves want and need.

The UNHCR' Global Trends 2015 shows that a growing number of refugees prefer to seek opportunities outside of refugee camps, away from encampment restrictions on movement, access to resources, ownership of assets and limitations on business activities. In light of this why do refugee camps persist?

Of course it is human nature not to wish to live a life on hold – to be left for years on end in a camp. We all aspire for a better life. The camps unfortunately persist due in part to the lack of willingness globally to provide resettlement places to those living there. They have nowhere else to go, they cannot return to the conflict zones but have no safe and legal routes such as resettlement to a more sustainable life either. This is why we are seeing so many people embarking on often dangerous irregular routes.

> One of the most chilling statistics appearing in the media relates to the number of the missing children – more than 10.000 according to Europol – which further stresses the urgent need for action. Which immediate actions are required to tackle this?

Early detection and triggering of protection procedures is key. The EU's Fundamental Rights Agency has also pointed to the problem that we do not have a fully functioning guardianship system in Europe, with each country operating a different system. What is very concerning is the cynical approach we see from certain politicians towards child rights in this situation. Some cite the 'anchor child theory' whereby children are sent alone with the sole purpose of abusing family reunification laws later. These allegations have never been backed up by any research. The sad reality is that war and conflict has created many orphans, led to families being separated. In addition to this and perhaps more importantly is, irrespective of the circumstances these children are highly vulnerable and have rights which are not being taken seriously enough by certain authorities. We need to treat every child as an individual with rights and have policies and practices that hold up their best interests given their particularly vulnerable situation.

The arrival of migrants and refugees has influenced the physical landscape of cities. Do you think that refugees and migrants should have a role in urban development planning in the host country?

Not something we would officially comment on.

1 internally displaced person
2 Amnesty International, 2016. *Refugees Welcome Index*. [online] Available at: https://www.amnesty.org/en/latest/news/2016/05/refugees-welcome-survey-results-2016/

"MAKING HEIMAT"
IS A VIRTUE
Guillem Pujol Borràs
Júlia Trias Jurado

At the beginning of the 16th century, Niccolò Machiavelli introduced one of the key concepts of modernity that contributed to building the idea that human beings are capable of engaging with their future, in contradiction to the prevailing God-centric notion of the time. According to the Florentine thinker, fortune was accountable for half of the actions of nature, whilst virtue was responsible for the other half. The former continued to be a force beyond human will, but virtue referred precisely to unique human skill. Machiavelli explained this through the following example: you cannot predict a storm (fortune), but you can build a dam to prevent the flood (virtue). Let's say for the sake of the reasoning, that Europe and its member states incarnate the symbolic figure of the Prince, the ruler who has the capacity to take the decision.

The political dysfunctional management in the current so-called refugee crisis challenges Machiavelli's thought. In 2015, more than 1 million people arrived in Europe by sea and 35.000 by land. In the same year, more than 3.700 died in the Mediterranean trying to reach European shores. So far in 2016, more than 250.000 people have entered Europe by sea and more than 3.000 have been

59

reported dead or missing. Europe is facing one of the biggest political crises in its history: after the relocation plan for a total of 160.000 people failed in that EU Member States didn't comply with their quotas, the EU externalized its borders with the EU-Turkey agreement, sending people to a country where there is no guarantee for the respect of human rights. Where did virtue go? How should a virtuous Europe react? Why is it relevant to create a new "Heimat" for the people arriving in our countries?

Starting with the latter question: if there is any ontological feature that defines human nature, it is its relational characteristic. We are a relational species: we exist to the degree that we recognize ourselves in others. There is no "Self" without the "Other". We learn, grow, and develop through mimicking, and we do that by using language, an inherited common knowledge. Avoiding "the Other" implies the negation of a constitutive part of ourselves, thus neglecting our intrinsic relational characteristic. Making Heimat addresses this same idea. In order to create a real Heimat it is not only necessary to provide the material needs such as a house, food and education, but also to generate an integrative narrative in which the newcomer can identify itself in it and feel "at home". This is why it is important to expand migrants and refugees' effective choices about their livelihoods. Making Heimat should incorporate mechanisms where the perspectives and intentions of both refugee and migrant communities would take a role, as well as their political context and outlook for solutions. Structuring participatory assessments taking into account age, gender and diversity approaches are essential for achieving a successful integration process.

The idea of creating a space of horizontal cooperation and popular participation within refugee and migrant communities responds to two essential aspects of a process of integration and of the creation of a Heimat: on the one hand, the self-identification of refugees and migrants within the host city and community, and on the other, the opportunity for the Heimat project to adapt to their potential needs and, by reinventing itself, achieve a successful process of integration. In this regard, the articulation of monitoring mechanisms with a space for migrants and refugees is important since they would allow both popular participation and their input as policy recipients. While "Heimat" refers not only to the inhabited physical space, but also to a place with emotional ties of belonging, it is essential that the beneficiaries can make their voice heard as one more actor of the project, within municipal authorities, civil society groups, and so on. These kinds of participatory programmes would help to have a more comprehensive understanding on the impact of policy and the changes that may developed, and, more importantly, they would be directed at the identification of the newcomers with their daily environment.

Yet building Heimat should not discriminate among individuals. Participatory programmes should also be open to local urban residents with similar needs in order to bring into line local standards and newcomers' heterogeneous objectives. While in some cases useful, separating the mechanisms performing a "Heimat" for newcomers such as migrants and refugees on the one hand, and on the other for local communities, does not conform with the same idea of "Heimat" since it may not construct a sense of belonging to the broader local community. More importantly, while institutional actors have an important role in this, they are the same migrants, refugees or local communities that need to be identified with a "home". And so, the articulation of participatory mechanisms is essential for a successful process of integration. Indeed, whilst the challenge ahead should be to conceive how to set up institutional and social mechanisms in order to create a new or second "Heimat" for migrants and refugees, it should also not be forgotten that this is to be directed towards the totality of the community. A virtuous Prince would understand that societies are formed by something else than merely the sum of all their individual members: namely, that there is a human need to symbolically identify with a safe place called home.

Anna Terrón

Cartha – What experience can you draw from your former or current professional positions with regards to EU urban development projects directed towards the integration of migrants and refugees?

Anna Terrón – According to my experience, local authorities are key actors for migration management. All over Spain, migrants have access to city registers, irrespective of their status. That's been of the utmost importance in recent Spanish migration history, when millions have arrived in a short period of time. Migrants immediately become city dwellers, and the city is their first space for interaction both with administration and neighbours. The quality of public spaces and public services are key points for newcomers' integration, as it is for the rest of the city's inhabitants. Inclusive cities keep public spaces open for all and promote citizen and neighbour interaction. I would see urban development as a powerful tool for that to be done.

Cities need the capacity (which includes financial resources but not exclusively) to strategically plan their responses to mobility-caused urban development challenges, such as the provision of public services and proactive accommodation programs for all. However, local authorities are too often neglected by national (and EU) migration governance, which is focused on border issues. Governing migration effectively to address the challenges of mobility and diversity requires getting cities on board.

63

> Heimat refers to the idea of creating a "new home" for refugees who have left their familiar environments, stressing the relevance of a successful integration process. Which policies should be included in an arrival city in order for refugees and migrants to identify it as their "heimat"?

This is a tricky question. In many cases, refugees have been forced to leave their own "Heimat". They're now just looking for shelter, understanding their own feelings and shaping a new life will take time for them. We all guess they want to stay and they wish to stay, but data shows that a majority of them have it in mind to go back to their cities. It will take time for them to work it out.

Having said that, welcoming programs are needed. Housing, child education and healthcare are services that need to be provided on their arrival, while employment is a key point for their social integration. Over these obvious and basic human needs there's also the need to feel safe and to feel at home, as you suggest. A proactive public policy is needed for that to be achieved. An intercultural strategy can be promoted both by local authorities and civil society for newcomers to be part of the community. Avoiding isolation and promoting participation and interrelation between newcomers and the host society is important for social cohesion. An example of this can be found in the anti-rumors strategy tested in Barcelona and now being developed in other cities. The strategy is making a difference for both newcomers and residents in being an active part of the integration process.

64

The world is undergoing a process of rapid urbanization. In 1950, less than 30% of the world's population lived in cities and towns. That figure is expected to reach 60% by 2030. How is it possible to conceal this phenomena in urban areas with important unemployment rates?

Cities can take advantage of migration, as they've been doing so for centuries. Migration has always been the driving force for cities to grow. The journey from rural areas to cities was first happening at national level and today it is an international phenomenon. Jobs are not there waiting for newcomers, as they never have been; local communities have to take advantages of increasing populations to create new economic activity, for the mutual benefit of newcomers and all the local community. Local authorities can promote it. Increasing diversity should be an asset for the city's position in the global economy of people constantly coming and going.

It is argued that illegal immigration should be combatted by opening up legal channels for entry. The benefits of this "legalising" are obvious for the migrants themselves but how could this strategy also benefit the host country?

Migration is the oldest human strategy to improve own life conditions and to give the best expectations to descendents. Globalisation is fueling it, people mobility is an increasing phenomena in the global world. Like it or not, it's there. We can manage migration or just let it happen. Managing migration is not only about border control. Managing migration means legal channels for entry and accommodation, and that's very important for hosting countries. It is about labor market and social policies, cities and housing, education, economic policies and economic strategy in the global market. The paradox of anti-migrants is that they do not prevent migration from happening, they worsen the conditions in which migration processes take place and they increase social tension related to it. Managing migration in a multilevel strategy which goes from local to international level is a more sensible option as long as it benefits host countries and countries of origin as well.

Beyond the need for EU Member States to comply with EU regulations and policies, you advocate for the need of an integrated immigration policy and reform of the common asylum system. What would this imply and what would be the benefits for refugees?

This so-called Common Asylum System does not establish an European framework for refugee protection, but instead represents an internal agreement concerning which country should examine an asylum application and under which criteria, and how it should ensure protection is offered in its territory when the application is approved. In other words, the European response to the international obligation of protection and asylum is rerouted to the national sphere and limited to a single default country. Without violating the division of powers, it is possible to go much further in the construction of the common asylum policy provided for in Title V of the Treaty on the Functioning of the European Union, which governs the Area of Freedom, Justice and Security. Moving towards "more Europe" means breaking past taboos and daring to establish a real and commonly governed European asylum system. This system could detach the review process for asylum applications (conducted according to pre-agreed criteria and procedures) from effective access to one or other (sub)systems of national protection. The question of where this right of protection would become effective could be determined later, and the joint responsibility of the different member states should be added to the list of determining criteria, and taking into consideration the cities and local authorities, which have a key role in welcoming and accommodating refugees. Such a system could eliminate incentives for non-compliance in countries and encourage newcomers to immediately apply, allowing better management of flows and avoiding secondary movements which engender serious repercussions for both newcomers, particularly the most vulnerable, and the larger society.

> "Terrorism" and "radicalism" are being increasingly related to migrants and refugees. What role do you think arrival cities can play with regards to this perception?

Perception is very important on migration issues, as it is on every single issue likely to be extremely divisive, in terms of "them and us". It is very easy

67

to amalgamate in a toxic narrative elements like migration, religion, and terrorism, whether the connections are proven or not, and even if causal relations cannot be established. Nonetheless, populist and xenophobic movements make the case for this relation in a very effective way and with a very dangerous outcome: they create new problems and do not solve the ones they pretend they are addressing. Internal and external security policies need to be developed at EU and international level to protect all of us. We do not have room here to develop this point. Just let me add that besides security policies, social action is needed to engage citizens, including newcomers in isolating terrorists, and terrorism as an option, especially among young people. Pretending they're all potential terrorists and representing them as such is precisely the wrong approach.

> Different concepts are used in order to describe different types of forced migration processes, such as economic migrant, environmental migrant, illegal migrants or refugees. What consequences do you think these differentiations entail?

From a legal perspective, there are two main regimes, economic migration for which states have discretionary power, and asylum, which falls into the sphere of rights protected by international legislation. I'm well aware that there's a thin line dividing both categories but I do think we must keep a privileged regime for those in need of urgent and effective protection under the Geneva convention.

That does not mean keeping migration on the dark side. As I said, we must manage migration.

The so-called "illegal migrants" are not a category at all, but we should discuss and cope with the fact that a number of asylum seekers and migrants will fall out of both categories. When repatriation is not an option we should find a way out. Protracted situations of legal limbo are dangerous for migrants in such situations and for hosting societies. Cities are especially concerned by this, as they have neighbours not recognized by the State but effectively living there.

> While it is argued that an efficient public transport service could help to undermine the risk of social exclusion of migrant and refugee communities, what other measures could be implemented in this regard?

I do think migrants should be seen in a city just as residents and neighbours are. The more the city and its urban public space promote inclusiveness and cohesion for all, the more it will ease integration processes. Over the very short term welcoming strategies to remove barriers and obstacles, all residents should be included in local services planning. In that sense, I do not think multiculturalism is a good strategy for local integration strategies, understanding it as a set of "communities targeted" public policies. The existence of high quality services and inclusive public spaces for all is the relevant question. Indeed, a proactive policy is needed to accompany newcomers on their way to effectively becoming city dwellers, that meaning public policies aimed to remove barriers for them to get access to services and to public spaces, making intercultural relations possible.

CROWDSOURCING HEIMAT?
Irena Guidikova

What the great imperial, commercial and intellectual centres of the world have had in common throughout history is the diversity of people they attract, and a talent for stimulating and managing cross-cultural exchanges. Their success is to a large extent due to what Charles Landry and Phil Wood have called the diversity advantage[1].

For centuries, human mobility and the resulting diversity of languages, religions, lifestyles, ideas and skills have been drivers of knowledge generation, growth and productivity. For the most part, these benefits have been the result of organic processes of inter-cultural mixing and interaction in the context of daily life. However, they have usually come at a significant human cost. Creativity and innovation have often been driven by friction and conflict between ethnic and religious communities, the expression of both a survival instinct and the will to succeed despite formal and informal barriers and exclusion mechanisms between culturally defined communities. Until a few decades ago, community cohesion was not an aspiration or even as a possibility, neither was dealing with cultural diversity seen as a task for public authorities.

Today governance, in particular at the local level, is (in principle) more informed, ethically enlightened and resourced than ever before: nations and

71

cities can use benign social engineering in order to reap the benefits of diversity while minimising its costs. But nations and cities are not equal vis-à-vis the demands of diversity management. While weakened nation-states tend to fall prey to populist leaders conjuring the cultural homogeneity of an imaginary golden age to mobilise voters' fear of change, cities embrace diversity as a motor of development. In urban centres, the *laisser faire* of old is increasingly replaced by urban diversity strategies in an attempt to counter the natural processes of segmentation and segregation that foster inter-group mistrust and animosity and accentuate socio-economic divides.

Even in countries with a strong multicultural tradition, a strong awareness is emerging of the need address ethnic segregation – both special and mental – and focus urban policies in creating mixed public spaces and inclusive institutions competent in managing intercultural relations in a proactive, positive way. Such awareness is welcome as in the multiculturalism's own showcase countries ideological and social divides run deeper than ever. More and more people lead segregated lives, only meeting and communicating with those who think like them. Pluralist, open-minded public space is shrinking.

Urban diversity and inclusion strategies are growing increasingly sophisticated and intercultural (it no longer makes much sense to speak about majority and minorities in cities like Geneva, London and

Amsterdam), less reliant on massive regeneration projects and iconic landmarks designed to attract strangers, not build communities, and more on fine-grain "eco-systemic" approaches involving inhabitants as architects and masterminds of their own place-making. The humbling of urban planners has coincided with the rise of community developers skilled in creating substantive dynamics connecting people around designing shared spaces which can foster a pluralist urban (neighborhood) identity and a sense of belonging. Some of these dynamics are so profound and sustainable that they effectively convert into lasting mechanisms taking cities into the dimension of participatory democracy.

We are just in the beginning to building a nuanced understanding of how such open-minded spaces emerge and the importance they hold for the local community. Publicly owned, flexibly defined in their function, sometimes managed by the users, these are spaces where unexpected and unplanned things can happen – from a flash mob to a pup-up civic agora, guerilla gardening: spaces where risks can be taken, where people can engage in doing things together rather than just talking, going over the barriers of language skills and low self-confidence.

Cities like Reggio Emilia in Italy and the London borough of Lewisham, when engaging in bottom-up neighborhood regeneration of "problematic" or unsafe areas (in many cases in the aftermath of traumatic events such as urban violence or racist

73

murders), have found that in order to ensure a democratic and inclusive process, it has been necessary to go door-to-door with interpreters, so that people of different backgrounds and levels of mastering the local language, could contribute to the consultation process and voice their concerns without having to take part in formal meetings. Making the effort (and the expense) of involving everyone in a more than formal community consultation not only sends a signal to residents that everyone matters, but also helps shape a project which resembles the local community in more than one way.

Some cities are even considering imposing a special "tax" on developers for an artist-led community engagement process throughout the entire urban regeneration process, instead of, as usual, involving artists as an afterthought, for superficial "embellishments".

Artists-led regeneration is a way of giving the city back to the citizens but also bringing the cities to the spotlight. Loures and Nuremberg involved famous graffiti artists in creating the mural paintings based on the stories and narratives of the inhabitants in the districts of Quinta do Mocho (Loures) and Langwasser (Nuremberg) in an attempt to change the image of these diverse and rather deprived neighbourhoods and give them a new impetus using diversity as a source of inspiration. These initiatives have successfully managed to change external (feeling of insecurity, fear of migrants) and internal (lack of self-esteem, lack of ownership) prejudice around the neighbourhoods. Such developments are inherently intercultural as they harness the creative power of diversity by intent, seeking to dig out and blend unique cultural perspectives and personal stores into a potent narrative of a pluralistic place which is happy to accommodate many different identities and be constantly redefined by its changing demographic realities.

In Lisbon the annual *Todos* festival reaches a new dimension in the always renewed interplay between urban fabric, landscape and creative energy. Each year the inhabitants of the diverse Mouraria district reinvent the present and the future of their neighborhood through the sounds, smells, histories, dreams and hopes of the inhabitants, offering an ephemeral experience of travelling the world within a square mile, but also shaping together the physical fabric of the neighborhood, which is after each edition enriched with urban art markers of the diverse makeup of the residents. People who live and work in Mouraria "collect" stories and memories of their neighbours, open the doors of their homes, workplaces and places of worship. Taking diversity very seriously, *Todos* empowers not only people of migrant background, but has special facilities to encourage the self-expression of those with disabilities too. Conceived as a crowd-sourced cultural happening of a new genre, *Todos* is both curated and organically grown, an art project and a social intervention, a community therapy and an exercise in participatory democracy, an urban laboratory which is inspiring other neighborhoods and cities in Portugal.

Designing Dublin (2010–2011) is perhaps one of the most far-reaching and iconic examples of crowd-sourcing the intercultural design of a city. Driven by the desire to revitalise a fledgling centre which had been deserted by the middle class, the city of Dublin launched a large-scale operation of social innovation in pace-making. The *Designing Dublin* team (including many volunteers from the city administration) started by trying to understand this phenomenon and then finding ways to make the centre a more vibrant, appealing and welcoming place for a wider and more diverse range of residents, visitors, urban enthusiasts, etc. Over several months the team reviewed the centre and its features, diversity, challenges, and opportunities. The project covered the entire social innovation cycle – "out of the box" thinking, desire to cross boundaries, intensive conversations with citizens of all kinds of backgrounds about their vision of the city and the features which would make the centre more attractive and welcoming (such as urban sofas and green corners in unexpected places), turning the best ideas into prototypes, real-life testing, and implementing those which were found to work. No effort was spared to reach out to those who are usually excluded (or self-excluded) from such operations. The project kick-started new urban dynamics and consolidated a culture of inclusive interculturalism, with the city council casting itself as a learning organisation tuned into the pulse of the community. One of the most striking realisations *Designing Dublin* triggered was that the best way to re-invigorate the city centre was to inspire people to step out of their routine and rediscover it in a new way through urban experiences that are unexpected, enthusing, challenging and pleasurable. In order to deliver such experiences, the city had to foster interconnectivity, collaborations, opportunities for social interaction, in other words, it had to practice interculturality.

Intercultural Heimat is pluralistic, open-minded, and in constant process of re-invention, it needs the interplay of diverse cultural references and inputs. An intercultural Heimat is almost a negation of Heimat as a collective – and collectivist – construction. It is the art of managing the city organically – using fine strokes to transform an ugly verruca where the urban skin has reacted to disruptive new arrivals, into an engine of vitality and development. It "takes a village" to design public institutions and public space which gently guide us into engaging with strangers, building connections, arguing, negotiating, making sense, making society.

References: Landry Charles and Phil Wood, The Intercultural City: Planning for Diversity Advantage, London, 2008
1   the diversity concept Landry, C. and P. Wood: 2008

Thomas Jezequel

Cartha – Asylum policy is a responsibility of national governments. According to the EUROCITIES report "Refugee reception and integration in cities", many cities have taken over from national authorities to set up reception measures for refugees. Can you put an example of how this can be conceived?

Thomas Jezequel – Cities most of the time do not have a formal legal role in receiving asylum seekers, but they had to act because nobody else did. There are countless examples of this. It is fair to say that national governments did not plan for the massive wave of arrivals which took place in 2015, and that no or very little measures were in place. But at city level, the belief that the refugee crisis would have a strong urban dimension was already there in 2014: cities like Milan or Athens were already telling us that they had to play a role normally devoted to national governments. This lead to the release of our "Statement on Asylum in cities" in spring 2015, a few months before the "Balkan Road" crisis saw the arrival of tens of thousands of asylum seekers in Vienna, Munich, Berlin or Malmö. These cities had to act quickly and beyond their mandate to avoid a humanitarian crisis. This response was made possible because Mayors showed leadership and empowered their administrations to act, also often playing a coordinating role of all actions at local level: the response of NGOs, public agencies, Civil Society Organisations and volunteers helped a great deal.

78

While one of the recommendations of this same EUROCITIES report is to housing refugees in socially mixed communities, the idea of "integration through segregation" argues that migrants find it easier to settle if they share space with people from their same community of origin. What is your opinion about this?

The trend at city level seems to be, and for quite a number of years, firmly against the idea that segregation can have a positive effect.

Much is done at city level to promote social mix, to deliver affordable housing in a time of austerity, budget cuts and adverse EU state aid rules. The refugee crisis makes this issue even more acute: the point of view that newcomers should be "dispersed" across neighbourhoods and communities at city level seems very mainstream to me, in cities receiving a few hundreds of refugees and cities receiving tens of thousands. This is not only a question of integration but also a question of social cohesion as a whole: as a decision maker and an elected politician it is much easier to defend desegregated housing, small shelters and individual apartments than massive refugee reception centres. It means that pressure on public services is balanced across the city and not concentrated on what particular neighbourhood.

According to the Integrating Cities Charter last report, some city policies are moving away from immigrant-specific services toward service provision for all residents, irrespective of their language, nationality and country of birth. If we consider that the process of integration should be bidirectional, what role do you think refugees and migrants should play in this regard?

There is always a trend going towards a "mainstreaming" approach, seeing social inclusion as the key and integration as outdated, but it is often counterbalanced by cities that move back to a more targeted approach. Nevertheless, the idea that all city services should have an integration dimension in mind is embedded into the Integrating Cities Charter: it is not up to a single integration department at city level to make integration work. Its task is to play a coordinating role and to make all services (Labour Market Inclusion, Housing, Culture, Education, etc) work together with the same objective and under the same principles. This is the so called "integrated approach", and a great added value at a local level.

The refugee crisis has an accelerating effect, and many cities are updating their integration plan to make it relevant to the new situation. "Integration from day one" is the new motto in many cities, meaning that city services do not wait for newcomers to receive a refugee status to start integration. This is about empowerment and maximising the chance of a quick and smooth integration into society.

What we've witnessed also in this new situation is that many asylum seekers and refugees are keen to self-organise into associations, collectives, interacting with civil society organisations and volunteers in host cities. City authorities often have a key role in "picking up" these initiatives, providing them with support, funding, or even making them part of the city administration, to ensure they can be made more sustainable and have a greater effect.

> While engaging public perception on migration and diversity and providing language courses are essential for cities to work towards refugee and migrants' integration, how could urban planning contribute to this aim?

Again this is about the way we live in cities that are increasingly diverse. This is a question of social cohesion, and of a city's role to promote social mix and avoid segregation. This is not only linked to the refugee crisis, but a more global question of demographic change and growing cities. Housing is one of the main challenges for major cities today, and the provision of affordable housing for all is very high on the agenda.

For many cities, the refugee crisis has put even more pressure on the availability of housing stock. This trend is likely to continue, as most recognised refugees will settle in cities.

The construction of new social housing for vulnerable groups such as refugees is not hindered by state aid rules. Nevertheless, an approach that focuses only on providing affordable housing for refugees and not to other vulnerable groups could lead to social conflicts and tensions. Giving newcomers access to housing in cities while lower middle class populations struggle to find decent and affordable

81

housing and are unable to access social housing will lead to resentment.

Furthermore, focusing on the delivery of social housing to refugees alone will cause segregation and risks creating ghettos. This will be detrimental to the social integration of refugees. Using public funds on housing for refugees while neglecting other parts of society is not a viable solution. A more flexible policy of providing affordable housing for all would enable cities and housing providers to play a crucial role in mixing newcomers with the local population.

> In a context of budget cuts and recruitment freezing in cities, is there a potential growing space for the private sector to invest in social housing and urban planning in view of integrating refugees and migrants?

More generally there is a growing space for non-public actors to play a role in the integration of newcomers. By this I also mean volunteers, civil society organisations, philanthropies, and of course the private sector. This is not a challenge that cities can face alone, and while we advocate for better multi-level governance (effective collaboration between cities, regions, nations and the EU) and direct funding for cities for integration matters, we are very conscious that public administrations will not deliver unless they work closely with other stakeholders at local level. This is not limited to social housing, where investment is in any case limited by EU State Aid rules as it must focus solely on so-called "vulnerable groups". Private sector involvement is obviously needed to strengthen the link between education and labour market inclusion, to improve vocational training programs, Cities have a key role to play in promote inclusive labour market at local level, as they can coordinate the efforts of all stakeholders.

One of the problems of the refugee and migrant crisis is the lack of support in certain countries. What can be done to encourage the support of hosting communities to host migrants and refugees from a city perspective?

Few topics illustrate as much as the refugee crisis how much cities and national governments diverge than when it comes to how they communicate about it. Over the last few years, many national politicians in the EU deliberately trumped up fears, resentment and rejection. Their narrative has been about border control and protection, terrorism and radicalization, protecting the homogeneity and "values" of the society, while pretending to do this to prevent the rise of even more populist parties.

This is of course problematic, but very often we see that major cities talk and act very differently from their national governments. There is no comparison between migration policies at local level in Birmingham, Bristol, Glasgow, Liverpool, London, Manchester, and the national discourse in the UK. Cities like Gdansk and Poznan in Poland, Brno in the Czech Republic, both in a very hostile political context, are working intensely on integration and diversity and want to be open to the world.

In cities where such leadership is demonstrated, and I mean political leadership and commitment by all levels of the administration, I firmly believe that perceptions can change and hosting communities can feel empowered to demonstrate support to migrants and refugees. The anti-refugee, anti-migrant, anti-diversity discourse is far from being mainstream in large cities in Europe, this is quite the opposite.

The recent open letter from European mayors members of EUROCITIES to EU leaders on World Refugee Day 2016 made it clear: *"There is too much talk of quotas, numbers and borders, and not enough of people. These are people who are fleeing war, persecution and destitution. How we treat them when they arrive in our local communities will determine the success of long term integration and social cohesion in Europe as whole"*

In each city, there are citizens acquired to the "cause" of refugees, whose response to the first mass arrivals was often overwhelming. For some of them, most of the time, the city does not do enough, and they keep their city council accountable. Some cities, in countries which did not receive as many refugees, reported that they were under pressure from citizens to act and prepare themselves to welcome more, for example in Barcelona or Madrid. There are obviously in some cities groups which are unequivocally hostile to refugees, migrants and diversity, and which will not be convinced otherwise. Cities still have to try to engage with these groups, at least to counter their rhetoric. But cities also and mainly have to communicate towards what has been defined as the "anxious middle". These are citizens whose concerns about newcomers must be heard and addressed in an open and transparent manner. Dismissing them and shutting them down will only feed rumours, resentment and fears, especially in a context where topics like terrorism and radicalisation are high on the political and media agenda. The objective are to build trust in the way authorities are dealing with the situation, and acceptance at city level in order to foster social cohesion and improve chances of integration for newcomers.

Integration policies in general and in particular all the work on public commitment to an inclusive and diverse society, awareness raising, challenging prejudices, defusing tensions, are nothing new for many European Cities. This is why they are the best placed to make integration happen and to promote a different narrative about welcoming migrants and refugees in our societies.

THE DESERT ON THE MARGINS IS MY HEIMAT: FOR A NON-EUROCENTRIC VISION OF MIGRATIONS AND ARCHITECTURE
Parasite 2.0

We explore the idea of migration with a non-Eurocentric perspective in the context of the current migration crisis as a starting point for the creation of a supranational state free from third-party governments, viewing peculiar radical islands such as the refugee camps as places where the concept of Heimat may be fully realised.

0. REPORTING FROM THE WESTERN FRONT
Nowadays, as Europeans, we are used to looking at migration movements with a centripetal perspective: from outside, overstepping a border, towards our prosperous continent. Over the centuries, the recognition of a limit – of an inside and an outside – thus led to the individuation of a different subject, "the other", which lies at the basis of the very concept of Europe as described by Braudel. This, in turn, triggered off specific narratives about nature, man and civilisation, resulting in the outright scission between East and West.

In *Orientalism* (1978), Edward Said tackles the issue of redefining and explaining the construction of the East by the Old Continent. According to Said, the East is not a practically identifiable geographical and cultural entity. On the contrary, he regards it as a tool employed by European cultures with the purpose of building their own identity as Europe, pigeonholing "other" cultures into simplistic stereotypes and generalisations.

Said neatly outlines the Eurocentric nature of the ideological imposition of the difference between East and West – a specious device that also played a crucial role in the achievements of Colonialism. Is it fair to say that our explanation of the real is almost completely based on a Western cultural experience? "Reporting from the front" – which front? With what eyes are we looking at this front? Who's responsible for its creation? Is the Western world really willing to aid those who, in our view, are no longer capable of mastering their existence? Is this aid ultimately directed towards another aim beyond?

1. SALVIFIC ARCHITECTURE

In recent years we have observed the return of a theoretical and practical trend that views architecture as having the possibility of solving political and/or social issues. We have seen a growth in the number of publications, biennials and projects on the topic, though uncritical ones sometimes, thus yielding to a general mystification of these concepts and of their meanings. Symptomatic of such a return is the renewed attention to the *Maison Dom-ino*, which turned a hundred in 2014 and has become an icon for those who believe in Open Source Architecture. Le Corbusier's project was born in response to a housing crisis in Belgium in order to provide dwellings in a situation of social unease; today, it still serves the same purpose for entire populations migrating towards Third World megalopolises. It is, indeed, the most prominent and widespread tool for architectural anarchy, being employed in a variety of scenarios ranging from the Favelas informal reality to North Africa, from "abusivism" in Southern Italy to Greek Polykatoikia. It is the symbol of that kind of architecture that developed between the two World Wars, at a time when the scarcity of houses in fast-growing or war-devastated cities prompted a great deal of architects to found the Modern Movement, whose pivotal tenet was the creation of the perfect city for the modern man: the demiurge-architect resembles god in its creative act, building an ethically charged theoretical structure with a supposedly central social role. Le Corbusier, with his insane idea for the Paris of the future, was the main advocate of this ideology and its contradictions. The modern project gave rise to a polarised city fragmented into social classes. Today, indeed, if we journey through the suburbs of the cities that were reached and modified by such theories, we can detect its by-products: the theories, transformed into political weapons aimed at resolving social tensions within the urban landscape, were applied according to principles of ostracism and exclusion.

The demolition of the urban housing project Pruitt-Igoe, with which Charles Jenks set the seal on the end of modernist utopia, provides a case study of the misleading use and failure of architecture whenever this does not operate with valid policies.

Indeed, the "modern experiment" attempted to export the European model of the city to other continents in which entirely different cultures and traditions were rooted. Examples include Le Corbusier's idealised and preposterous Algiers plan, and the Candilis, Josic and Woods' "Nid D'abeille" project in Casablanca. Here the European failure to export and westernise "the other" is apparent.

2. SIDE EFFECTS AND RADICAL ISLANDS

The Modern Movement urbanism stirred up a process of urban estrangement of those lower classes that were born out of urban cleansings such as Haussmann's "Grand Travaux" in Paris and the "Plan Cerdà" in Barcelona. Such projects have promoted the formation of cities fragmented into different social classes, while simultaneously encouraging the creation of urban radical islands, which harbour the potential to rebel, where it is possible to imagine new codes of ethics. They testify to the disingenuous, if not deceptive, nature of urbanisation processes that masquerade as major works for the redevelopment and improvement of social conditions. Haussmann's healthy, bright and spacious Ville Lumière is a city made for the Boulevards' burgeoning bourgeoisie – not for all. It can be classed as one of the first examples of Urban Regeneration – a word that today's architects prefer to the out-of-

-favour gentrification, though it does not really move away from it. In these two cases, the side effects are particularly noteworthy: on one hand, the Paris Commune; on the other, Catalan anarchism (also to be found in other Spanish regions) during the Spanish Civil War. In 1901, in the working-class district of Atochas Monte Alto (La Coruña, Spain) a priest married two women, which was the first same-sex marriage in history. In the bowels of anarchic Barcelona, the first naturist schools began to appear, where a free and open vision of knowledge could be transmitted, escaping the oppression of the Catholic establishment, the only source of education at the time. This goes to show how "*it's a paradox that the places thought to be the most uninhabitable turn out to be the only ones still in some way inhabited. An old squatted shack still feels more lived in than the so-called luxury apartments where it is only possible to set down the furniture and get the décor just right while waiting for the next move. Within many of today's megalopolises, the shantytowns are the last living and livable areas, and also, of course, the most deadly.*"[1]

The idea of the island and the desert – intended as springboards for the formulation of new worldviews – has been explored, historically, by numerous writers and philosophers. In "Causes and Reasons of Desert Islands", for instance, Deleuze talks about continental islands, harking back to the definition given by geographers to accidental or drifting islands, which originate from a fracture in the mainland – an erosion that chase them away, a

90

detachment that labels them as different and foreign bodies. By the same token, in 1516, Thomas Moore attempted to elude the censorship of his time by devising an imaginary island by the name of Utopia, also coining this word. The island, by representing an antithesis to England under Henry VIII, embodies new codes and ethics in a potential different world. Can we look at these places of exclusion, at these artificial desert islands as the only places left where an alternative to the status quo can be envisaged, where architecture can retrieve its social, political and ethical role?

3. RADICAL ISLANDS, REFUGEE CAMPS AND THE STATE OF "OTHER" TERRITORIES

"Our task will be to protect cultural and existential spaces that allow us to prepare the conditions for the time after this one, of violence and misery, that we have now entered, I believe, irreversibly. Our task will be to create survival spaces and to sabotage colonial predation and war. The problem will concern the forms of prosperous survival: which dimension can they find and how persistent can they be? To what extent will they succeed in connecting with experiences of institutional representation? To what extent will they succeed in envisioning projects to come?"[2]

Refugee camps are radical islands scattered throughout that contemporary metropolis that spreads out on the whole Mediterranean area and that is now expanding on a global scale. As it was

91

for Catalan and Parisian districts of exclusion that were subsequently turned into places for collective experimentation, it is perhaps through the lens of today's refugee camps and their frontier condition that we can rethink the concept of the migrant, beginning with these margins where new communities strive to form day after day, each one settling in with its own cultural codes.

In his recent book "Mondi Possibili" (Possible Worlds), Marco Petroni, starting from Said – who saw the migrant as a key twentieth-century figure, "with no homeland, […] situating itself amid several territories, forms, houses" – describes how contemporary economical and social dynamics have erased the exceptionality of the nomadic condition, while leaving it as "the only possible way to lay claim to one's own subjectivity in a context of ever-lasting global crisis."[3]

"It is within this in-between dimension that the paradigm of the possible – understood as transformation project, remoulding of the world – comes into play. The design of the possible operates in multiple directions, in an area of continual transit of cultures, social and individual stories. 'Living on borders and in margins – Chicana poet Gloria Anzaldúa claims – keeping intact one's shifting and multiple identity and integrity, is like trying to swim in a new element.'"[4]

Petroni maintains that "the design of the possible", which moves through borders and margins, is the only way to shape a "renewed social role" and to redefine designers as "translators of meaning". In some refugee camps, we have seen the birth and growth of alternative ways of dealing with collective life and economy, with the result of recovering concepts of solidarity, exchange and gift, in stark contrast to capitalist accumulation. In a sense, these places already offer examples of "the design of the possible".

Calais is perhaps the most representative case. Today the so-called jungle hosts around 3.000 migrants, who are trapped in limbo for entire weeks or months. The camp, which almost violates human rights, has risen autonomously following the dismantlement and closure of another refugee camp in Sangatte. Now there rise small self-managed schools and service systems that are supported by activists and volunteers. Some fringes of architecture and political activism have become interested in these places in a similar way to how, in recent years, informal urbanism such as the favelas had attracted their attention. We need to be careful, however, not to charge these case studies with excessive radicalism, lest we mystify them through rhetorical theorisations.

In 2016, in the small city of Gioiosa Ionica in Calabria (deemed to be one of the most problematic regions in Southern-Italy) the municipality welcomed a group of asylum seekers. In a town of only 7.000 people, such a proposal was accompanied by a project that may at first sound like a joke, but ultimately displayed a great potential. A group of

93

activists invented a sort of alternative currency, whose notes feature famous communist leaders' faces. This currency, in agreement with local shopkeepers, was then given out to the migrants who could then use it within the town. The idea, reminiscent of current experiments romanticised by libertarian thinking such as Bitcoin, has had a remarkably positive impact both on the asylum seekers' living conditions and on local economy.

If the refugee crisis can generate forms of horizontal and caring economies, why shouldn't we also imagine new social policies or even new forms of government? If we were to compose a map of the Heimats – of the refugees' Heimats –, could we then form a state and write its constitution? A system of codes with which to envision a new world. Can the world itself start afresh from there? We imagine a supranational state of which refugees can be citizens and in which the concept of Heimat can be realised most meaningfully.

1   The invisible committee, The coming insurrection, (Los Angeles: Semiotext(e), 2009), p. 72
2   Franco Berardi (Bifo), "Un convegno perché" http://effimera. org/un-convegno-perche-di-franco-berardi-bifo/ [translated by Lorenzo Mandelli]
3   Marco Petroni, Mondi Possibili. Appunti di teoria del design, (Milano: Temporale, 2016), p. 90 [Translated by Lorenzo Mandelli]
4   ibid., p. 91

Loren B. Landau

Cartha – The world is undergoing a process of rapid urbanization. In 1950, less than 30% of the world's population lived in cities and towns. That figure is expected to reach 60% by 2030. To what extent should public institutions take into account migration processes in the development in their urban plans?

Loren B. Landau – In this day and age you are not making an urban plan if you are not considering mobility's varied forms. With the dissolution of permanent employment and the stripping away of state support for the poor and marginalised, mobility is an ever more normalised part of human life. We are increasingly aware of the global elite's movements among sites and often celebrate their ability to forge connections and communication. While the effects of 'ordinary' mobility are likely to be different, such movements are central to achieving people's social and economic aspiration. Cities must adapt. This is not only about translocal service provision, but considering new modes of economic planning, budgeting, and civic participation.

Heimat refers to the idea of creating a "new home" for refugees and migrants who have left their familiar environments, stressing the relevance of a successful integration process. Which policies should be included in an arrival city in order for refugees and migrants to identify it as their "Heimat"?

In an era of heightened economic precarity and social fragmentation, it is difficult to even ask who has

95

the authority to make policy or the ability to structure an integrated social world. Rather than the previous generation's churches, unions, and civic clubs, integration now is far more social, privatised, and flexible. Indeed, we are increasingly seeing integration in motion; a kind of fluid form of coming together. This is not based on promises of a common culture or political values; but rather on modes of getting along in ways that facility ongoing flexibility and mobility. Some would argue this is a kind of minimalist integration based on an acceptance of multiculturalism. To some extent that is true. However, if we separate civic identity from social identity, we can actually see this as immigrants and hosts – whoever they may be – authoring their own rules and forms of civic engagement. If we accept that immigrants have a right to be in the space we have previously occupied, then we must also accept their right to negotiate belonging as they choose. Our responsibility – as planners or policy makers – is to identify the structures and interventions that incentivise exclusion. With those limited or removed, people can construct their own civics; their own heimat.

> In terms of cultural identity integration, there are two differentiated approaches, multiculturalism and cosmopolitanism. Which model do you think arrival cities should follow for a refugee welcoming policy?

In their very nature, cities are diverse spaces. Such diversity can be the source of productive tensions and dynamic translocal and transcultural collaborations. Yet substantial challenges exist for building and governing cities in which populations' orientations and trajectories extend primarily beyond city "walls". This is not a question of demanding unfailing loyalty to a state or city or trying to fix people's bodies or minds in space. This is not a question of achieving social cohesion at the cost of varied opinions and conflict. Rather, what is needed is the ability to foster multiple forms of engagement. So while we often speak of people expressing their social identities in multiple, sometimes contradictory registers, we must now too think about politics as a practice on multiple planes. This may require not so much a cosmopolitan identity, but a recognition that people's lives are shaped by obligations and contributions at multiple levels.

"Citizenship" is related to a set of rights in a given State. Do you consider, as other scholars, that this concept is harmful for newcomers?

Citizenship is exercised on multiple levels. Across much of the world – and indeed in Europe – the scale of the sovereign state is losing its relative importance in practical and normative terms. Instead, people participate politically – accessing rights, influencing social life, shaping policy – in multiple spaces. These include the highly local sites of clubs and community to the transnational world of the European Union, the Umma or global pentecostalism. Each of these scales continues to influence each other and individual lives in ways that are dynamic and mutually constitutive. Those concerned with building inclusive communities and citizenship must recognise that forms of integration and belonging can be forged in multiples spaces simultaneously. While restrictive forms of national citizenship continue to generate exclusionary socialities and cities, there are increasingly opportunities to erode and circumvent such restrictions.

What specific characteristics should social housing have in order to contribute to the integration of refugees and economic migrants?

An answer to this question is premised on what we understand what constitutes the goals and processes of integration. If we work from a classical definition of joining an existing host community, it must be affordable, diverse, and stable: a basis for building socialities that extend beyond ethnic and national categories. However, if we accept that successful livelihoods often demand flexibility, translocality, and ongoing movements, social housing must be created in ways that allow for people to restructure their social and economic exchanges in multiple ways. This will demand multiple forms of housing provision that can accommodate varied family structures, residential patterns, tenure systems, and communal engagements.

Given your expertise in Africa's urban spheres, is there any experience that could be translated into

European integration policies?

What we're increasingly seeing across African cities is a kind of Do It Yourself Urbanism. This stems from economic and demographic changes that rapidly outpace formal structures' ability to respond. Without the disciplining and integrating forces of expanding formal employment or state institutions, people have been free (or forced) to forge their own forms of sociality and politics. While the history and politics of African cities create many informally governed spaces, this may well be the future for cities across Europe and elsewhere in the world. Whether it's the peri-urban banlieus in France or new immigrant enclaves across other European cities, there are increasingly sections of cities which remain at once part of and removed from the city; governed – in part or in whole – by logics of transience and translocality.

The process of "Making Heimat" is to be accomplished by both the arrival country and the immigrants themselves. What role do you think refugees and migrants should play in their process of integration?

The primary driver of integration – building new forms of sociality and civic engagement – will always be refugees and migrants themselves. A country or a host population cannot integrate someone; at best they can create conditions in which 'the other' can form bonds, instrumental relations, or tactical disengagements. While host countries may have the ethical bases to shape the initial meeting between

99

foreigner and citizen, the very act of accepting them into "your" space is a recognition that from that point in time, the space is shared and will be shaped by the incentives, interests and interactions that follow.

BEING AT HOME IS NOT WHAT IT USED TO BE[1]
After Belonging Agency

In the domestic interiors of a Brutalist council estate, new fabrication technologies coexist with laminated wood furniture, neon-colored drones, souvenirs from remote territories, faux animal prints, and leather sofas. It is mid-afternoon. Shots of colorful parrots and Capuchin monkeys interweave with scenes of teenagers who, while sitting in front of TVs displaying international channels, communicate through phones and laptops, share images with close and distant friends, and place orders online. 3-D printing alternates with hookah smoking. Jeans and leggings are combined with smiling-face-printed niqabs; hoodies, with Afro-punk-patterned bomber jackets. Japanese kanji tattoos cover arms and backs. These scenes depict a weekday in Peckham, South London, the home of communities with diverse origins from all over England and from East Asia, South Asia, the Caribbean, Africa, the Middle East, and Eastern Europe.[2]

The scenes in these spaces exemplify a larger condition. In 2015, the online retailing company Alibaba shipped 12.2 billion packages to home addresses.[3] The social media platform Instagram contained 58.940.079 posts tagged #home.[4] According to recent reports, more than 240 million people are living in a place where they were not born,[5] while

101

the number of tourist arrivals throughout the world – stays of less than twelve months – is over one billion.[6] Contemporary spaces of residence are shaped around the circulation of goods, images, and individuals moving throughout wider territories. Pervasive commercial exchanges, systems of information transfer, and migratory movements have destabilized what we understand by residence, forcing us to question spatial permanence, property, and identity.

Being at home has different definitions nowadays – both within domestic settings and in the spaces enclosed by national boundaries. New modes of being at and constructing home are entangled with a contemporary reconfiguration of belonging. Understood both in relation to our bonds to places and collectivities, as well as to the changing attachments to the objects that are produced, owned, shared, and exchanged, belonging is no longer just something constrained to one's own space of residence or to the territory of a nation, nor does it last an entire lifespan. Belonging is being contemporaneously transformed at different scales and in different contexts. For example, the daily life of the middle classes around the world is being reconfigured by the economic conditions and social relations enabled by home-sharing platforms, as well as by the production of aesthetic regimes mobilized in the postings on these platforms. And yet, the universal ambitions advertised through Airbnb's motto, "Belong Anywhere," is in stark contrast to the bureaucratic realities of how such belonging is, in fact, regulated by local laws which determine the movement of the users of these home-sharing platforms between countries.[7]

The processes of globalization have brought greater accessibility to ever-new goods, fueled alternative imaginaries, and provided access to further geographies and knowledges. And yet, not everybody moves voluntarily, nor in the same way. The global regimes of circulation grounded in changing geopolitical relations, the uneven developments of neoliberalism, and the expansion of media technologies, also promote growing inequalities for large groups, kept in precarious states of transit. Despite the expansion of circulatory processes affecting domestic spaces, contemporary international events suggest a reinforcement of borders, economic protectionism and political autarchy, attempting to resist the effects of globalization – from the 2014 Australia's government anti-immigration ad campaign declaring "No Way. You will not make Australia Home;"[8] to the results of the United Kingdom's European Union membership referendum; the border fences erected by European countries and in countries like Jordan as a result of the so called refugee crisis;[9] U.S President Donald Trump's executive order on immigration affecting millions of refugees and citizens of seven Muslim-majority countries, and the building of the southwestern border wall with Mexico proposed by his administration.[10] Major institutions and established architecture

103

platforms, such as the recent Pritzker Architecture Prize, awarded to RCR architects, have even reflected on this trends by stating: "We live in a globalized world where we must rely on international influences, trade, discussion, transactions, etc. But more and more people fear that, because of this international influence, we will lose our local values, our local art, and our local customs. They are concerned and sometimes frightened."[11] From the scale of the residence to that of the country, the construction of the space of the home – and the homeland – seems to define lines of division and conditions of inclusion and exclusion.

While the aforementioned geopolitical transformations seem to reinforce the concept of the nation-state as a geographically confined site of belonging, other phenomena support alternative arguments: President Trump's immigration ban unleashed protests across the globe and a surge in donations to groups like the American Civil Liberties Union;[12] progress on the development of the all-African passport will soon allow many to expand the territories they can call home;[13] and, on a darker note, the Islamic State has recently proclaimed itself to be a worldwide caliphate, with religious, political and military authority, presenting a religious inflection of the nation-state.[14] Moreover, the dissemination of information and images increasingly shared in social media builds imaginaries and shapes aspirations that continue to fuel the movement of people: the number of teenage boys

104

migrating from Egypt – a country that is not currently indexed as suffering a civil war – after receiving images and narratives of success from friends and family members via social media, has reached unprecedented levels, to the point that some parts of the territory are almost devoid of their youth.[15]

These shifting and seemingly opposed conditions (of apparent territorial isolation and stabilization, and contradictory geopolitical reconfigurations) have architectural manifestations and effects in our modes of being at home and spaces of residences. Furthermore, belonging, as architecture, is simultaneously concerned with physical and social spaces. It addresses questions of affection, technological transformations, material transactions, and economic processes. And, at all of these levels, belonging is neither good or bad, yet it remains as a contentious concept. By analyzing the ramifications of this concept and its relation to material manifestations at different scales, it is possible to propose and advance new ways of understanding architecture's transformed relation to enclosure and stability, and therefore, alternative notions of what being at home might or could be. Place-making and the construction of a sense of identity constitute only the most typical among other possible agendas for which architecture could be mobilized. Architecture has served over time for diverse, often opposed, ideological endeavors of belonging: it has been crucial in constructing and vindicating national identities as a symbol for liberation from colonial and imperialist forms of power, but has also supported essentialist projects. By critically inspecting how architecture is articulated towards specific ends in the transformation of belonging, other possible trajectories for architectural production emerge.

In a time defined by mobility and transit, the the various definitions of the house characterized by the most canonical architectural expressions of residence and belonging are destabilized, and the seamless construction of homeliness as a solid unity grounded in intimacy, privacy, and rootedness are questioned. Instead, the house could be considered as an unstable aggregate of objects, bodies, spaces, institutions, technologies, and imaginations. Contemporary architectures of housing are enmeshed in the logics of real estate speculation, many of them connected to territorial processes of massive urbanization and global migration, and increasingly transformed by technological mediations, while continuing to appeal to different traditions and ambitions of stability. In the midst of transcontinental migrations, newly-imagined landscapes, and financial speculation, traveling constituencies continue to make themselves at home in different conditions: for example, Norwegian retiree resorts along the Spanish Coast, in which architecture mediates the advantage of the chosen location with aesthetic and material links to the community of origin.

We could also consider the different understandings of residence as they relate to the legal definition of citizenship and as a form of cultural binding to a territory and a nation, and speculate on architecture's articulation with different kinds of "imagined communities" that have become substitutes for the family and religion as the primary forms of social stabilization in technologically advanced, neoliberal, global contexts.[16] And yet, the nation, family, and religion still continue to take new forms in these contexts, with architecture decidedly participating in their articulation. For example, the contested sovereignty of airport spaces – and their complex role in the filtering of individuals and objects – is in some cases countered by a decided effort by nations to present themselves as cohesive units to communities in transit. New techno-spatial articulations are also operating in transnational congregations of religious communities such as those of Charismatic-Pentecostalism in sub-Saharan countries.

In order to understand these new manifestations, a new approach is needed different from the structuralist impulse to relate the architectural forms of the house with social practices in different global contexts.[17] Rather than exploring isolated architectural productions in relation to their local contexts (reinforcing traditional forms of belonging), this new approach requires to understand the cultural, technological, and material links – whose effects have been variously described as "freak displacements," "disjunctures," and "frictions" – configuring the different spatial articulations of

107

contemporary culture.[18] The house, in these contexts, no longer relates to phenomenological ideas of place or community stability, but with "the estranging sense of the relocation of the home and the world in an unhallowed place" that many have explored through the condition of the *"unheimlich"* (unhomely) and through postcolonial studies.[19] The architectures built with remittance money arriving to different Latin American countries, for example, perfectly illustrate this condition. But this case manifests how the sense of home and the uncanny condition of contemporary forms of residence exceed the aesthetic problem of representation of both individuals and communities, aiming to make themselves at home in different architectures. Indeed, there are specific bodies at stake here, as well as specific resources and material transactions. And while money, in this case, seems to travel swiftly between the nations of emigration and immigration, technical knowledges are modified in their translation between the two for the construction of these characteristic architectures, and individuals are often trapped by borders, or have their defining forms of citizenship change while crossing the border.[20]

The architectures associated with the aforementioned transactions and operations sometimes entail the definition of a homogenous landscape. On other occasions, the architectures respond to the construction of differentiated (or decidedly differentiating) representations of identity for diverse geographical contexts or "imaginative geographies" within this global landscape.[21] In some cases they result in material boundlessness, while in others they are manifested in the definition of material boundaries.[22] Considering these changing forms of identity construction, distributions of property, and constructions of enclosure is as far from the advocacy of nomadism, as it is from the celebration of a return to local traditions and rooted communities. Many critical projects exploring nomadism in the last decades have been grounded in the pursuit of a cosmopolitan, secular society, freed from local ties.[23] However, the same mobility that these projects celebrated has been coincidental with neoliberal regimes that have led to the precarization of labor, massive concentrations of wealth, and dispossessed populations kept in transit. Similarly, the construction of home, or a sense of home, has been many times followed by the design of separating barriers that manage the flows and passage of bodies, information, goods, whether they are conceived at the scale of the house, or that of the territory: from door lockers, safe rooms and gated communities, to the architectures of seasteading, the design of autonomous enclaves, and security border walls.

And yet, other forms of architectural practice offer new forms of engagement with our contemporary changing realities, and challenge distinctions between inside and outside between host and guest. The development of such project and intervention strategies was one of the goals of the Oslo

109

Architecture Triennale 2016: *After Belonging*. For example, Open Transformation, a project developed within that context, proposes innovative systems for meeting asylum seekers needs and "intervene in the larger process of displacement derived from global migration, including real estate market forces and housing solutions."[24] Their application bnbOPEN, presented as an alternative or supplement to reception centers, would enable the newly arrived to find and share ordinary housing with the local inhabitants. Similarly, an abandoned fruit orchard on the edge of the Oslo *Tørshov Transittmottak*, a transit center for refugees and asylum seekers from wars in Syria, Afghanistan, Iraq and other countries, is the site of a project by Eriksen Skajaa Arkitekter. The architects, after analyzing how this site is used by the residents at the centre as a free source of fresh fruit, as an area for collective action, consequently designed an architectural device: an apple press. Constructed together with the local community, the apple press is a space where new collectives become possible through the harvest, and where the inhabitants could go beyond the dualism between the need for intimacy and the need to take part in the collective life and dense living quarters in the facility.[25] Another example of how architecture and architects could contribute to the definition of alternative spaces of belonging and inclusive imaginaries of home is Matilde Cassani's design for Prato's gonfalone – a type of heraldic flag and traditional symbol of identity for every Italian commune and municipality. Located in the vicinity of Florence, Prato currently has one of the biggest Chinatowns in Europe, with more than 50.000 inhabitants (more than half allegedly without work permits), and one of the engines for the manufacturing of "Made in Italy" labeled products which the industry proudly sells throughout the world as a trademark of quality based on "local" standards of production. Together with representatives of the local institutions, and using as a starting point the existing gonfalone and its language, Cassani actualized the collective memory of the city in accordance with the changing needs of the contemporary world, and its new local identity.

These projects and positions address and imagine the architectures of new constructions of belonging, new ways of being together, new collectivities, and inclusive architectures of the home, where other transactions, connections, and solidarities to occur. By questioning universal and traditional notions of home, as well as a nostalgic search for a lost understanding of belonging, these architectures foster alternative forms of cooperation and cohabitation, identity construction, distributions of property, and constructions of enclosure which in turn have the capacity to transform the attachments between individuals, and the relation between communities and the territory. That is, the spaces and conditions that define the "being at home."

After Belonging Agency is composed by Lluís Alexandre Casanovas Blanco, Ignacio González Galán, Carlos Mínguez Carrasco, Alejandra Navarrete Llopis, and Marina Otero Verzier

1   An earlier version of this text was published in the Introduction to *After Belonging: The Objects, Spaces, and Territories, of the Ways We Stay in Transit*, Lluís Alexandre Casanovas Blanco, Ignacio G. Galán, Carlos Mínguez Carrasco, Alejandra Navarrete Llopis, Marina Otero Verzier eds. (Zurich: Lars Müller Publishers, 2016), 12-23.

2   Description of scenes in the Sri-Lankan-born British singer M.I.A.'s music video "Double Bubble Trouble." "Double Bubble Trouble" is a song from the album Matangi (2013), written by Maya "M.I.A." Arulpragasam, Ruben Fernhout, Jerry Leembruggen, and Rypke Westra, produced by The Partysquad, and released on May 30, 2014.

3   Alibaba Group Holding Limited, "Annual Report for the Fiscal Year ended March 31, 2016," p. 77, http://www.alibaba-group.com/en/ir/ pdf/form20F—160525.pdf.

4   https://www.instagram.com, accessed June 5, 2016.

5   United Nations, Department of Economic and Social Affairs, Population Division,"Population Facts:Trends in International Migration, 2015," December 2015, accessed May 24, 2016, http://www.un.org/en/development/desa/population/migration/publications/populationfacts/docs/MigrationPopFacts20154.pdf.

6   United Nations World Tourism Organization, UNWTO Annual Report 2015 (Madrid: United Nations World Tourism Organization, 2016), 2, http://cf.cdn.unwto.org/sites/all/files/pdf/annual—report—2015—lr.pdf/.

7   Brian Chesky, "Belong Anywhere," Airbnb Blog, July 16, 2014, http://blog.airbnb.com/belonganywhere/.

8   Oliver Laughland, "Australian government targets asylum seekers with graphic campaign," *The Guardian*, February 11, 2014, https://www.theguardian.com/world/2014/feb/11/government-launches-new-graphic-campaign-to-deter-asylum-seekers

9   These fences challenge the free movement of individuals established by the Schengen Treaty. "The Schengen area and cooperation,"EUR-Lex, last modified August 3, 2009, http://eur-lex.europa.eu/legalcontent/EN/TXT/?uri=URIS-ERV%3Al3-3020. Rana F. Sweis, "Jordan Closes Border to Syrian Refugees After Suicide Car Bomb Kills 6," *The New York Times*, June 21, 2016,http://www.nytimes.com/2016/06/22/world/middleeast/jordansyria-attack.html?—r=0.

10 Design-Build Structure. Solicitation Number: 2017-JC-

RT-0001. Agency: Department of Homeland Security. Office: Customs and Border Protection. Federal Business Opportunities website, February 24, 2017; https://www.fbo.gov/index?s=opportunity&mode=form&id=b8e1b2a-6876519ca0aedd748e1e491cf&tab=core&—cview=0

11 "Rafael Aranda, Carme Pigemand Ramon Vilalta Receive the 2017 Pritzker Architecture Prize," Announcement, The Pritzker Architecture Prize, March 1, 2017: http://www.pritzkerprize.com/2017/announcement

12 Iiam Stack, "Donations to A.C.L.U. and Other Organizations Surge After Trump's Order," *The New York Times*, January 30, 2017, https://www.nytimes.com/2017/01/30/us/aclu-fund-raising-trump-travel-ban.html?—r=0

13 Anne Frugé., "The opposite of Brexit: African Union launches an all-Africa passport," *The Washington Post*, July 1, 2016, https://www.washingtonpost.com/news/monkcy-cage/wp/2016/07/01/theopposite-of-brexitafrican-union-launch-esan-all-africa-passport/.

14 "The legality of all emirates, groups, states, and organizations, becomes null by the expansion of the Khilāfah's authority and arrival of its troops to their areas." Abu Muhammad al-'Adnani al-Shami, "This Is the Promise of Allah," video transcript released by Jihadology.net / Al-Hayat MediaCenter, June 19, 2014, accessed July 8th,2016, https://ia902505.us.archive.org/28/items/poa—25984/EN.pdf/.

15 Declan Walsh, "Facebook Envy Lures Egyptian Teenagers to Europe and the Migrant Life," *The New York Times*, June 23, 2016, http://www.nytimes.com/2016/06/24/world/middleeast/facebookenvy-and-italian-lawlurc-cgyptian-teenagersto-europe.html/.

16 The expression "imaginary communities" was famously coined by Benedict Anderson in his work on modern nationalism. Benedict Anderson, *Imagined Communities*, rev. Ed. (London and New York:Verso, 1991).

17 See, for example, Pierre Bourdieu, "The Berber House or the World Reversed," in *Social Science Information 9*, no. 2 (1970) and the more general arguments by Amos Rapoport, "Sociocultural factors and house form," in *House Form and Culture* (Englewood Cliffs, NJ: Prentice Hall, 1969).

18 Homi Bhabha, "The World and the Home," *Social Text 10*, no. 2 (1992); Arjun Appadurai, "Disjuncture and Difference" in *Modernity at Large: Cultural Dimensions of Globalization* (Minneapolis: University of Minnesota Press, 1995); Anna L. Tsing, *Friction: An Ethnography of Global Connection* (Princeton, N.J.: Princeton University Press, 2005).

113

19 See Bhabha, "The World and the Home," 141–2: "The un-
    homely is the shock of recognition of the world-in-the-home,
    the home-in-the-world. Although the 'unhomely' is a
    paradigmatic postcolonial experience, it has resonance that
    can be heard distinctly, if erratically, in fictions that negotiate
    the powers of cultura difference in a range of historical
    conditions and social contradictions." The notion of the un-
    canny, originally a Freudian notion, has additionally
    been linked by Julia Kristeva to an analysis includes both one's
    own other as well as an understanding of the stranger as
    part of one's own self. See Julia Kristeva, *Strangers to Ourselves*
    (New York: Columbia University Press, 1991), 181–2.

20 As Jacques Derrida has problematized, subjects do not carry
    rights and duties during their physical transit: these
    are continuously negotiated at each side of the border line.
    See Jacques Derrida, *Of Hospitality: Anne Dufourmantelle Invites
    Jacques Derrida to Respond*, trans. Rachel Bowlby (Stanford,
    Calif.: Stanford University Press, 2000).

21 Edward W. Said, "Imaginative Geographies," in *Orientalism*
    (London: Penguin, 1978).

22 Gilles Deleuze reported from the work of Felix Guattari how
    we might live in "a city where one would be able to
    leave one's own apartment, one's street, one's neighborhood,
    thanks to one's (dividual) electronic card that raises a
    given barrier; but the card could just as easily be rejected on
    a given day or between certain hours; what counts is not
    the barrier but the computer that tracks each person's position
    – licit or illicit – and effects a universal modulation."
    Gilles Deleuze, "Postscript on the Societies of Control,"
    October 59 (Winter 1992): 7.

23 Edward W. Said, for example, understood the potentials
    of exile as a form of freedom from local ties and detachment
    from orthodoxy. "The exile knows that in a secular and
    contingent world, homes are always provisional. Borders and
    barriers, which enclose us within the safety of familiar
    territory, can also become prisons, and are often defended
    beyond reason or necessity. Exiles cross borders, break
    barriers of thought and experience." Edward Said, "Reflec-
    tions on exile," [1984] in *Reflections on Exile and Other
    Essays* (Cambridge, Mass.: Harvard University Press, 2000),
    147.

24 See Open Transformation, a project developed by Elisabeth
    Søiland, Silje Klepsvik and Åsne Hagen for the In
    Residence Program of the 2016 Oslo Architecture Triennale,
    After Belonging: http://oslotriennale.no/en/torshov

25 See, Eriksen Skajaa Arkitekter "The apple orchard at Torshov

reception centre," in *After Belonging: The Objects, Spaces, and Territories, of the Ways We Stay in Transit*, Lluís Alexandre Casanovas Blanco, Ignacio G. Galán, Carlos Mínguez Carrasco, Alejandra Navarrete Llopis, Marina Otero Verzier eds. (Zurich: Lars Müller Publishers, 2016), 196-197

26 See *Living Outside the Walls: The Chinese in Prato*, edited by Graeme Johanson, Russell Smyth, and Rebecca French (Newcastle upon Tyne: Cambridge Scholars Publishing, 2009).

27 Manufacturing Assemblages in Prato, In Residence, Oslo Architecture Triennale (OAT) 2016, *After Belonging: A Triennale In Residence, On Residence and the Ways we Stay in Transit*, OAT website: http://oslotriennale.no/en/manufacturing See also "Sewing machines, dragons, watermelons and firecrackers," project by Matilde Cassani and commissioned by the Oslo Architecture Triennale 2016, Matilde Cassani website: http://www.matildecassani.com/#myCarousel31

BIOGRAPHIES

Oliver Elser
Born 1972 in Rüsselsheim. Studied architecture in Berlin. From 2003 to 2007 architecture critic and journalist in Vienna. Curator at the Deutsches Architekturmuseum (DAM) since 2007 and author of numerous articles for newspapers, magazines, and books: 2012/13: Associate Professor of scenography at FH Mainz. Exhibitions include: *The Architecture Model – Tools, Fetish, Small Utopia*, 2012; *The 387 Houses of Peter Fritz* at Venice Art Biennale, 2013; *Mission: Postmodern. Heinrich Klotz and the Wunderkammer DAM*, 2014.

Peter Cachola Schmal
Born 1960 in Altötting. Father from Munich, mother from the Philippines. Has lived in Multan/Pakistan, Mülheim/Ruhr, Germany Jakarta/Indonesia, Holzminden, and Baden-Baden. Studied architecture at the TU Darmstadt. Worked at Behnisch+Partner in Stuttgart in 1989 and from 1990 to 1993 at Eisenbach+Partner in Zeppelinheim. From 1992 to 1997 Assistant Professor at the TU Darmstadt. From 1997 to 2000 taught architectural design at the University of Applied Sciences in Frankfurt am Main. From 2000 curator, and from 2006 director of DAM. German commissary general for the 7th International Architecture Biennale in São Paulo in 2007.

Anna Scheuermann (née Hesse)
Born 1977 in Lahn-Giessen. Studied architecture at TU Darmstadt and Tec de Monterrey, Querétaro, Mexico. 2005/06 trainee at DAM. Since 2006, freelance curator and author. Co-curated the German entry for the 7th International Architecture Biennale in São Paulo in 2007. Since 2007, press and public relations work for various architects and engineers. Exhibitions include: *schneider+schumacher*, 2012; *Nove Novos*, 2013; *Suomi Seven*, 2014.

Saskia Sassen

She is the Robert S. Lynd Professor of Sociology, and Chairs The Committee on Global Thought, Columbia University. She is a student of cities, immigration, and states in the world economy, with inequality, gendering and digitization three key variables running through her work. She has received many awards and honors, among them multiple doctor honoris causa, the 2013 Principe de Asturias Prize in the Social Sciences, election to the Royal Academy of the Sciences of the Netherlands, and made a Chevalier de l'Ordre des Arts et Lettres by the French government.

Brandlhuber+

text by Brandlhuber+; Olaf Grawert, Anna Yeboah

Brandlhuber+ is a collaborative architectural practice based in Berlin. It was founded by Arno Brandlhuber in 2006.

Arno Brandlhuber

Studied Architecture and Urbanism at the TU Darmstadt and the Accademia del Arte in Florence. From 1992 on he initiated several project- and office partnerships, amongst others with Zamp Kelp and Julius Krauss, with Bernd Kniess (b&k+) as well as with Markus Emde and Thomas Burlon (Brandlhuber+ Emde, Burlon).

Since 2003 he holds the chair of architecture and urban research at the Academy of Fine Arts, Nuremberg and is directing the nomadic masters program: a42.org. He was a guest teacher at several universities including TU Wien, ETH Zurich and Harvard Graduate School of Design.

Besides his building practice he is researching the spatial production of the Berlin Republic, including several exhibitions and a recently published book on Berlin entitled The Dialogic City – Berlin wird Berlin.

His work has been included in the 9th, 10th, 11th, 13th and 15th Architecture Biennale. The latter showed the collaborative film Legislating Architecture by Brandlhuber+ Christopher Roth. As part of this ongoing research Brandlhuber+ Christopher Roth are currently investigating the topic of landownership by their current project: Legislating Architecture – The Property Drama.

Giovanna Borasi
Joined the CCA as Curator for Contemporary Architecture in 2005 and became Chief Curator in 2014. With a background in architecture, she initiated her career as an editor and writer, recently as Deputy Editor in Chief for Abitare (2011–2013) and for *Lotus International* (1998–2005) and *Lotus Navigator* (2000–2004). Her exhibitions and related books shape contemporary discussion in architecture with a particular attention to alternative ways of practicing and evaluating architecture, and how environmental, political and social issues are influencing today's urbanism and built environment: *Environment: Approaches for Tomorrow* (2006) on the work of Gilles Clément and Philippe Rahm, *Some Ideas on Living in London and Tokyo by Stephen Taylor and Ryue Nishizawa* (2008), *Journeys: How Travelling Fruit, Ideas, and Buildings Rearrange our Environment* (2010), and *The Other Architect* (2015). She co-curated *Other Space Odysseys* (2010), *1973: Sorry, Out of Gas* (2007), *Actions: What You Can Do With the City* (2008–2009), *Imperfect Health: The Medicalization of Architecture* (2011) and *What About Happiness on the Building Site* (2017).

She has written widely on contemporary architecture, has served on international juries, and is a regular speaker at symposia and conferences.

Alfredo Brillembourg
Co-founder of interdisciplinary design practice Urban-Think Tank (U-TT), holds a joint Chair of Architecture and Urban Design at ETH Zürich. As co-principle of U-TT, he has received the 2010 Ralph Erskine Award, the 2011 Holcim Gold Award for Latin America,

the 2012 Holcim Global Silver Award, and was part of the Golden Lion-winning team at the 2012 Venice Biennale of Architecture. He has edited and contributed to a number of books, including *Informal City: Caracas Case* (2005), and *Torre David: Informal Vertical Communities* (2012).

Hubert Klumpner

Co-founder of interdisciplinary design practice Urban-Think Tank (U-TT), holds a joint Chair of Architecture and Urban Design at ETH Zürich. From 2013–2015, he served as the Dean of the Department of Architecture. As co-principle of U-TT, he has received the 2010 Ralph Erskine Award, the 2011 Holcim Gold Award for Latin America, the 2012 Holcim Global Silver Award, and was part of the Golden Lion-winning team at the 2012 Venice Biennale of Architecture. He has edited and contributed to a number of books, including *Informal City: Caracas Case* (2005), and *Torre David: Informal Vertical Communities* (2012).

Alexis Kalagas

Writer, researcher, and publications manager at the Urban-Think Tank Chair of Architecture and Urban Design, ETH Zürich. He co-edited the recent book *Reactivate Athens: 101 Ideas* (2017), has guest edited three editions of *SLUM Lab* magazine, and is currently working on a forthcoming book on low-cost housing in South Africa. His writing has also appeared in *Architectural Design, a+t, Perspecta, Journal of Visual Culture, trans magazin*, and the edited volume *Re-Living the City: UABB 2015* (2016).

David Harvey

Distinguished Professor of anthropology and geography at the Graduate Center of the City University of New York (CUNY). He received his PhD in geography from the University of Cambridge in 1961. Harvey has authored many books and essays that have been prominent in the development of modern geography as a discipline. He is a proponent of the idea of the right to the city.

Iverna McGowan
Acting Director of Amnesty International since 2012, overseeing the organisation's work towards the European Union (EU) and the Council of Europe (CoE). She holds an LL.M in European and International human rights law from the University of Maastricht, and a B.A. in European Studies from Trinity College Dublin.

Guillem Pujol Borras
Political Philosopher. Graduated in Political Science and MSc from the University of London, Birkbeck College in European Politics and Policy, Guillem is currently a PhD Candidate in Philosophy, where he studies the links between psychoanalysis, power, and urbanism.

Júlia Trias Jurado
Political Science graduate and is currently pursuing a Master of Arts in Refugee Protection and Forced Migration Studies at the School of Advanced Studies, University of London. Júlia works at Irídia – Centre for the Defense of Human Rights and as an external consultant in public policies related to refugee and migration issues.

Anna Terrón
President of InStrategies and Special Advisor to Commissioner Cecilia Malmstrom on migration issues. Ms. Terrón has been Special Representative of the Union for the Mediterranean Secretariat (2013–2015). She has also been Former Secretary of State for Immigration and Emigration of the Government of Spain (2010–2011) and former Secretary for the European Union of the Generalitat de Catalunya and the Catalan Government Delegate to the European Union

(2004–2010). She has been a member of the Committee of the Regions (spokesperson at the Commission on Citizenship, Governance, Institutional and External Affairs) and member of the European Parliament (1994–2004).

She is also a professor on migration policies at Blanquerna University (Barcelona). She holds a BA in Political Science and Public Administration.

Irena Guidikova

A graduate of Political Science and Political Philosophy from the Universities of Sofia (BG) and York (UK), she has been working at the Council of Europe since 1994. Her carrier started at the Directorate of Youth and Sport where she developed and carried out a large research programme, through a transversal 3-year project on the future of democracy in Europe producing standards on e-governance and e-voting, party financing, internet literacy and an agenda for the future of democracy in Europe. She then worked at the Private Office of the Secretary General where she was a policy advisor, and is now Head of Division at the Directorate of Democratic Governance, overseeing programmes on urban policies for intercultural integration and media and diversity. Since 2013 she is in also charge of the organisation of the annual World Forum for Democracy organised by the Council of Europe on issues relating to democratic innovation, bringing together over 1500 decision-makers, activists, journalists and academics from all over the world.

Thomas Jezequel

Policy advisor in charge of migration & integration at EUROCITIES, the network of major European Cities. He coordinates EUROCITIES' migration & integration working group and represents the network within the EU Urban Partnership on the inclusion of migrants and refugees. He has published for EUROCITIES several reports on the integration of migrants and refugees in cities since the start of the refugee crisis. Before his current position, Thomas Jézéquel worked for Caritas International Belgium on voluntary return policies, or the Hungarian Helsinki Committee on asylum in Central and Eastern Europe and for the Istanbul Refugee Law Aid Programme on asylum law.

Parasite 2.0

Founded in 2010 by Stefano Colombo, Eugenio Cosentino and Luca Marullo. They investigate the status of human habitat from the margins of conventional practice, acting within a hybrid of architecture, art, and social sciences. They are the 2016 winners of the YAP MAXXI. They have recently published the book Primitive Future Office. They are Assistant Professors at the Politecnico di Milano and NABA Nuova Accademia Belle Arti Milano.

Loren B Landau

Director of the African Center for Migration and Society (ACMS) (formerly Forced Migration Studies Programme, FMSP) at Wits University in Johannesburg, South Africa. With a background in political science and development studies, his work focuses on human mobility, development, and sovereignty.

After Belonging Agency

It is a group of architects, curators and scholars based in New York and Rotterdam, who came together specifically for the 2016 Oslo Architecture Triennale (OAT) and is composed by:
    Lluís Alexandre Casanovas Blanco
Chief Curator, OAT 2016/Princeton University
    Ignacio G. Galán
Chief Curator, OAT 2016/Principal [igg – office for architecture]/Term Assistant Professor, Barnard+Columbia Architecture
    Carlos Mínguez Carrasco
Chief Curator, OAT 2016/Associate Curator Storefront

for Art and Architecture
    Alejandra Navarrete Llopis
Chief Curator, OAT 2016/Principal NaMi
    Marina Otero Verzier
Chief Curator, OAT 2016/Head of Research, Het
Nieuwe Instituut

Contributors
Saskia Sassen
Brandlhuber+
Giovanna Borasi
Alfredo Brillembourg
Hubert Klumpner
Alexis Kalagas
David Harvey
Iverna McGowan
Guillem Pujol Borràs
Júlia Trias Jurado
Anna Terrón
Irena Guidikova
Thomas Jezequel
Parasite 2.0
Loren B. Landau
After Belonging Agency

Interviews
Pablo Garrido Arnaiz
Francisco Moura Veiga
Guillem Pujol Borràs
Júlia Trias Jurado

Graphic Design
Début Début
Max Frischknecht
Philipp Möckli

Proofreading
Lily Mcnulty-Bakas
Esther Lohri

CARTHA
Editorial Board
Elena Chiavi
Pablo Garrido Arnaiz
Francisco Moura Veiga
Francisco Ramos Ordóñez
Rubén Valdez

Institutional Support
Fundação Serra Henriques

Efforts have been made
to correct factual and grammat-
ical errors and to standardize
typographical elements.
Eccentricities of language and
phrasing have been retained.

Printer
DZA Druckerei zu Altenburg
GmbH

Font
Lexicon by Bram de Does

Paper
Alster 175 80gm2,
Alster Cover 240gm2

www.carthamagazine.com
info@carthamagazine.com

Publisher
Park Books
Niederdorfstrasse 54
8001 Zurich
Switzerland
www.park-books.com

Park Books is being
supported by the Federal Office
of Culture with a general sub-
sidy for the years 2016–2020.

ISBN 978-3-03860-053-4

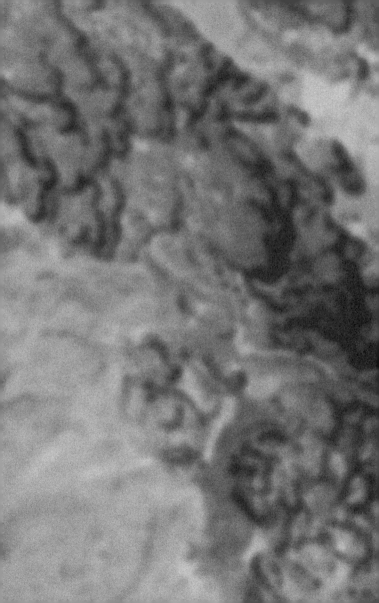